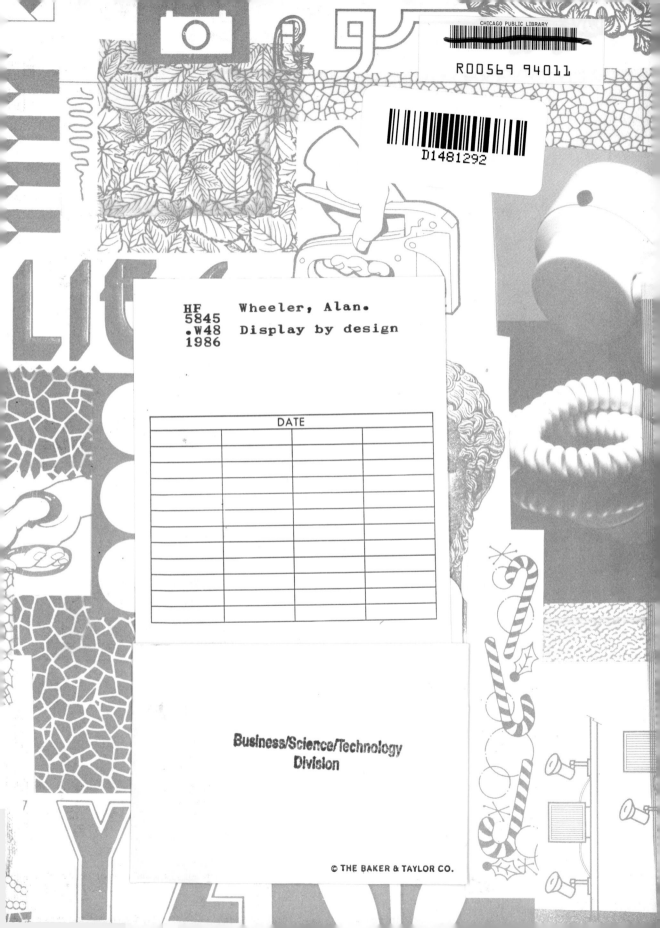

Display by Design

Alan Wheeler

Cornwall Books
New York · London · Toronto

For Gillian
Ross and Fleur

© 1986 by Rosemont Publishing and Printing Corporation

Cornwall Books
440 Forsgate Drive
Cranbury, NJ 08512

Cornwall Books
25 Sicilian Avenue
London WC1A 2QH, England

Cornwall Books
2133 Royal Windsor Drive
Unit 1
Mississauga, Ontario
Canada L5J 1K5

Library of Congress Cataloging-in-Publication Data

Wheeler, Alan.
    Display by design.

    Bibliography: p.
    Includes index.
    1. Display of merchandise. I. Title.
HF5845.W48 1986   659.1′57   86–19620
ISBN 0–8453–4802–7 (alk. paper)

Printed in Great Britain

Contents

Acknowledgements

My gratitude and thanks to Sarah Manson for asking me to write *Display by Design*; to my wife and children for their patience; and finally, and most important, to my typist and friend Sylvia Marnham, who deciphered my scribbles and jottings and delivered every chapter on time and with a smile.

I would like to thank the companies and individuals listed below for their co-operation with research and visual material. Arthur Stewart-Liberty, Liberty; Gene Moore, Tiffany; Paul Muller, Liberty; Harry Wyeth, Jaeger; Hugh Coe, London Institute (CDT); Roy Gentry, Liberty; Alan Harvey, Thorntons; Ivan Monty, Propaganza; Walter Kilb, Ricemans; Shirley Harris, Oxfam; Adel Rootstein; David Wilkinson, *Daily Telegraph*; Janet Turner, Concord; Iris Webb; Dennis Miller, *Daily Telegraph*; Anthony Wilson; Ivan Tremayne, Sandersons; Alan Mason Watson, Weekes; Charles Hammond; Gary Withers, Imagination; Ron Jones, Selfridges Oxford; David Hawcock; Ronald Barton; Fiona Wylie, Next; Wiggins Teape; Sylvia Morton, Jetmaster; Paul Swain, Turnbull and Asser; Georgia Landless, Elizabeth Arden; Catherine Brighty, Brighteyes; Derrick Woodward; Muriel Brightmore; Graham Sweet; Judith Boniface, Stransky Thompson; John Giles, Marler Haley; Major Charles Fenwick, The Chelsea Gardener; Alec Smithers, Royal Doulton; Chorley Floral Products; Screenplan; Alternative Designs; Browns of Chester; John Lewis Partnership; Richard Stevens; David Edwick; Woking Paper Tubes; Jackie Bogve.

Foreword

When I got back to Liberty's at the end of the war in 1946, I knew nothing about shop-keeping. However one thing seemed clear to me and that was the vital importance of shop windows in a retail business. I had been taught in the Army, that however little one knew about soldiering one could at least assume a soldierly appearance and a clean face on parade. It is the same with shop windows, they are the face of the business and on this basis it is judged.

I therefore asked the Directors to allow me to attend a course on window display at the Reiman School in the Horseferry Road. They were surprised and a little disapproving. Window display was thought to be a matter for the selling staff and not really of sufficient importance to be the concern of a Director.

On my return from Horseferry Road, Arthur Symonds, the Editor of *Display* magazine, was kind enough to introduce me to Eric Lucking and I persuaded the Directors to appoint him as the first Display Manager at Liberty's. Before then display had been thought of as a departmental matter not requiring centralised control. Eric Lucking's work on the shop windows from then on enabled him to set a higher standard in terms of wit and imagination than had actually been arrived at in the merchandise in the store. In that way the shop windows acted as a catalyst to the whole business; the buyers and merchandising managers realised that the shop windows were creating a stir, and this in turn compelled them to buy merchandise which would live up to our new and improved reputation.

Alan Wheeler worked at Liberty's as a display man and participated in the excitement and stimulation of this period of development. That experience, his display work elsewhere, and his work as a lecturer at the College for the Distributive Trades have led to *Display by Design* and eminently qualify him to write it.

A. I. Stewart-Liberty

1: Introduction

I once smiled to myself in a lecture when I heard exhibition display referred to as industrial theatre. With hindsight I can see the true significance of the speaker's words: our high streets and malls would be dull places indeed without the skills of display teams.

The word *display* in itself conjures up many different images. We can link it to a setting out of work in the conference centre or classroom, the mounting of a museum exhibition, the decoration of a domestic or theatrical interior, or even the planning of a fancy dress party. A number of these areas are explored or referred to here but the chief aim of this book is to discuss display as seen in the merchandising or commercial sense — in shops, stores, malls, or market stalls, where presentation is an essential part of selling.

In today's highly competitive market-place, trading policies and a company's image are of prime importance. Since displays are the silent salesmen working day and night to promote our interests and since they represent our street image, they are vital if our name is to be respected and our merchandise sought after in the market-place. So now more than ever we are discovering that the display person or team is consulted and involved with the total merchandising programme.

Departments cannot or should not work in isolation. What purpose is served by a brilliant advertising campaign blazing a trail of which the rest of the organization is unaware? There is a real need now for companies to get their act together and make sure that the entire organization, large or small, is working towards the same ends. When this happens, the effect is amazing. On the retailing scene we recognize at once those stores or groups of stores and shops which have achieved unity in their approach to business. Of course the processes involved are many and in this volume I am interested only in the visual aspects of a merchandising programme. House style, advertising, and public relations are closely linked to the image of any retailer but displays are there twenty-four hours a day, every day of the year, showing our face to a passing public.

Preceding page: Grouping of everyday items by the author to demonstrate simple method of creating a spray painted background.

Having said this, I must add that style or image is an elusive quality. Top designers may imprint a product or company with their ideas and actions so that stationery, carrier bags, logos, and graphics may all co-ordinate beautifully. It is not quite so easy, however, when the display or three dimensional factor is approached. Ideas and visuals that look good on paper do not always translate into physical settings. This, then, is why the practical display feasibility of the scheme should be considered and a display person consulted in the initial stages.

With many modern shops and store designs, architects and shop fitting groups create truly beautiful fascias and interiors. Open plan and closed in display areas are an integral part of the whole. Showcases and merchandising units are often part of a modular system. However, the display team can come up against some impossible tasks by serious oversights on the designers' part. For instance, I have on different occasions sought desperately for a fixing from which to suspend something to find that I am searching in vain. So, when it comes to the actual realisation of an otherwise theoretical project or promotion, the more the display person's expertise is consulted, the more hassle and frustration can be avoided.

You will have noted by now that I have referred to display people with several different terms. What do we call ourselves? Labels such as *window dresser* (Britain) or *window trimmer* (America) are really rather out of date and limit the range of the job. *Display man* or *woman* sounds workmanlike; *display person* covers everything. I like personally the two expressive titles currently in use, *visual merchandiser* (America) or *display designer* (Britain).

One of the display person's activities is setting up and arranging scenes and groups of merchandise, or accessorizing live models for a photographer. This person is known as a *stylist* and can work freelance, be attached to any number of companies, or work solely for one photographic studio or publishing company. The stylist does not just set up a shot, but may be responsible for finding the necessary materials or for hiring anything from a candlestick to an artificial or real garden. The good stylist, therefore, has contacts and addresses for practically everything from artisans, who can paint backdrops, age furniture, and create headdresses or fantasy clothes, to model makers, mould makers, and firms selling every conceivable type of raw material.

I have been involved in many styling assignments and could never tell beforehand what surprises the sessions would bring. I remember one case where we had set up a whole studio for a large American cosmetic company. The models were dressed in exotic oriental costumes. Sand was strewn across the floor, with wind machines at the ready, and we had hired two stuffed cheetahs from a taxidermist. The idea was that the models should be standing and lying in a group with the cheetahs on gold chains, all very theatrical. After a couple of hours, the photographer, who had been flow over from New York to London for the session, decided that he wanted live cheetahs or failing that leopards. So a frantic phone call was put through to the London Zoo.

With the evergrowing fields of television, entertainment, and advertising plus the relatively new areas of pop and promotional videos, the sky's the limit for the creative display person. To me this is what makes the job exciting and a continual challenge. A florist is mainly involved with the many aspects of arranging beautiful blooms and foliage. The interior decorator is choosing colours, textures, and fabrics. Both these are exciting and creatively rewarding jobs but the role of the visual merchandiser or stylist is always changing. We never know what the next assignment will bring, we can never truly rest on our laurels. This for me keeps the job alive and interesting, and, unlike some other creative careers, the work carried out is completely transitory, ephemeral by its very nature, apart from some permanent displays in museums. We are as good as our last job and all that remains is on film or in our folios as pictures.

Looking back through files and addresses of work, reading write-ups and press cuttings of past jobs, I realise the tremendous amount of experience, the amazing range of skills and techniques, accumulated almost unknowingly, through working in the display arena.

Display is one very vital and visual part of the pattern of retailing but we all of us at sometime in our lives need to present ourselves, our work or skills, and our ideas not only verbally but visually.

Here, then, are just a few other places that can benefit tremendously from someone with a working knowledge of display techniques. This is not to imply that experts in their own chosen field are not capable or competent to organise such areas but the specialist, be it florist, chef or craftsman, cannot always gauge or plan for the big effect or the overall image.

In many hotels, for instance, once the interior designer has done his or her job and the champagne opening is over, the effects so lovingly brought about are all too often left to fade away and die. Colour schemes, display showcases, flowers, plants — all must be kept up meticulously. This is done by various individuals, but the result of each one completing their own tasks can be a visual equivalent of musicians doing their own thing with no conductor. A trained display person would be on the ball and pull the whole effect together. There are many locations, and events taking place within a hotel that could utilize someone with a display background. Information panels, mobile exhibitions, trade openings or conventions — all these could benefit from someone who is visually aware and used to creating effective schemes.

Wedding receptions, banquets, special thematic parties, galas, even restaurants — all rely so much on presentation. Once again the food, flowers, decor, and entertainment need to be co-ordinated and presented as a piece. All too often each section is looked after by a team or individual, who has no idea of the finished effect that the whole ensemble should or could make.

The display of food itself is a whole area of presentation with special rules. In certain countries we know that the preparation and arrangement is as important as the food itself. The clever chef will have laboured long and lovingly over his dishes, but sometimes the whole effect can be ruined by poor lighting, an unsympathetic choice of colour for background, and such like. I have attended quite palatial receptions, tables resplendent with superb dishes and bedecked with gorgeous flower pieces, only to cast my eyes further down to badly creased damask table coverings. Display know-how would have made sure that this simple task was carried out before a single item was placed on the tables.

Other aspects such as obtaining different heights and levels for large displays of many flat dishes come easily to the display person. Indeed our working lives are spent thinking of how we can obtain various levels in any given area.

I have mentioned a few environments where good display will help those who use it well. We do not need actual merchandise to sell to have interesting displays. Ticket agencies, travel agents and bureaux, hair dressing salons, real estate agents, and public libraries can all use the display man's skill and use them to good effect. In this country libraries are making exciting areas within their buildings where events, displays, and competitions happen regularly. Themes are introduced and to this end readers' eyes and minds are opened up, hopefully leading them into new and untried areas. I have given many demonstrations to bookshop and library personnel on using display ideas and themes with books. On every occasion I found the staff enthusiastic about making their work that much more interesting.

A knowledge of display techniques can be very useful to any teacher, expecially those lecturing or instructing on subjects that are essentially visual. From our earliest days at school we all of us can remember how exciting it was when teacher put our work on show. From the simplest projects such as leaf or potato printing, to student projects involving diagrams, charts, folders, samples, and models, all work gains from good presentation.

The schoolroom or any educational situation is no place to compete with the large stores or professional expertise. This is not what we are about, we want to make the children's or adults' work more interesting. Our displays should highlight solutions to problems, skills, and the mastering of techniques. We should group carefully and wherever possible have clear outlines as to the teacher's intent or hopes for the assignment.

Screens, panels, and shelves can all be found and brought into use. Remember that in many cases the actual tools and equipment used for work can make a decorative, interesting, and atmospheric contribution to the display. Items such as silk screens, rollers, brushes, looms, spinning or potters' wheels, carpentry tools, paints, easels, and machines can add another dimension to art and craft exhibits.

If your problem is that you have a number of folios or book type projects to display, and these are intended to be glanced at or opened, then tie your display materials up to the general or to a specific theme. Pictures, posters, maps, objects, or materials can relate in some way to add more impact and bite to what might be a dull corner. There are obvious links for example, projects on the sea could be placed on shells, pebbles, sand, and fishnet; historical essays might be set against old maps, documents, and faded or stained boards or fabrics. Actual costumes might be found to link your exhibits.

In places such as school or college exhibitions or diploma shows, the public must be led, guided, or intrigued into studying the items on show. Customer flow patterns are used widely in business, very often the same techniques can be used in other locations.

Do not forget that the entrance to any exhibit or area where a display is staged is very important. Use a bit of showmanship. All too often a student or member of staff sits or stands by a typical school table asking visitors to sign in and handing out leaflets or programmes. Make a feature of your show. Tables can be covered and transformed. Flowers and plants — real or artificial — can give a lift very easily. Whilst giving a group of pottery and ceramic students a day course, I discovered that there was an abundance of beautiful shrubs in the grounds surrounding the building. After a few words with the gardener, the teachers and I came back laden with laurel and rhododendron leaves along with many other varieties. At once the pots and vases sprang to life filled with or just laying or standing on the dark green bed of foliage.

Materials need not be costly. Lengths of battening or poles can be nailed, glued, or lashed together to form structures, ceilings, canopies, or stalls. Educational materials can be used in unusual ways. Desks, boards, and tables can be stacked, covered and re-grouped to give height or define areas. Our aim is not only to attract and interest parents and the general public but in setting up such exhibits to give children or teenagers a glimpse of how important the art of presenting our work and ourselves really is.

So display can help in several areas other than in a purely retail setting. The skills once learned are never lost or forgotten and as I look back over the lists of students and friends, I find that they seem to make or find a niche almost anywhere. Currently we have past students working in such places as Madame Tussauds, The National Theatre, Scotland Yard, local government offices, nursery schools, garden centres, hotel chains, B.B.C. television, and craft markets, and as florists, magazine stylists and photographic assistants. One of my former students runs his own company. One of his recent projects involved transforming the Orangerie at Versailles into a multi-level restaurant to stage a thousand-seat banquet with international cabaret support.

I want the reader to realise the full potential of the display person's craft. It can help us in so many ways. More and more these talents are being set free from the shop window and showroom and are blossoming forth with spectacular results in public places, enlivening otherwise dull events or occasions.

2: Autobiography

It would be a lie to say that I was artistic as a child. I can remember hating the geometric patterns which I was forced to draw and colour in the art room at school. When later I attended art school, I found this enjoyable but somehow not rewarding. However, I responded to the classes in fashion drawing with enthusiasm, and this, along with the influence of my mother's love of fabrics and the decorative arts, decided me to link art with commerce and enter the display field. My mother, some years previously, had worked with the couture house of Worth in Mayfair, designing and executing exquisite embroideries with silks, pearls, and jewels. I had sat for hours as a young child watching her plan these intricate designs on silks and chiffons, playing with her scraps of fabrics as if they were toys.

My own beginnings in display go back to the late 40s. I can remember as a young apprentice holding pins for senior staff, hoovering, and polishing glass with methylated spirits for hours on end. The display man's role has changed much since those post war days. In the small department store where I learned my craft, we wore suits with stiff white collar and tie. In the heat of summer we were allowed cream linen jackets, but the tie remained. Staff training was geared to the old school of thought that no matter how rude, arrogant, or offensive, the customer was always right. Although there were managing directors and floor managers, it was the buyers who really shaped and controlled the smaller stores. Larger than life they ruled the roost and in most cases much more. Sales staff were at their mercy, and like Tom Brown bullied by Flashman, they took their vengeance out in devious ways, sacking or reducing to tears those who crossed their paths.

It was the buyers in most department stores who were solely responsible for selecting the merchandise in their chosen departments. They too were at risk and the job carried a lot of worry and headaches. They would part from their beloved

Preceding page: display by the author for the business section of the *Daily Telegraph* window. Background uses a spray technique through cut-out stencils to suggest a city skyline. The head was made by A S Wilson from stiff white paper. Red carnations, clip boards, and a base of newspapers complete the mood.

hats or babywear, handing it over with great reluctance and dire warnings to the display person involved.

'Handle those hats with tissue, Mr Wheeler, they are French models. . . No pins please, those scarves are pure silk chiffon and if they come back damaged the display department will have to pay.'

These last words struck terror into our young hearts as budgets and salary were very low.

The one important thing that these years of rules and discipline engraved into my mind was, that I had to be organised. Like a chef prepares his working surfaces and lays out his ingredients, so the display person prepares himself.

Though hard to take those three years gave me a grounding that I could have learned no other way. Dealing with buyers, managers, and the public taught me that if one could discuss rather than demand, if one could interpret and anticipate the others' needs, then everyone seemed happier. This is a lesson we should never forget. There is no room for the prima donna in a display team. Individuality and, of course, allowances for artistic temperament and integrity must and can be made. However, it is also a great asset to establish good liaison with clients and to form an understanding and quick appraisal of situations and schedules of work to be done. When weighing up the problems of space, light, and the many other aspects involved in a proposed display, time is of the essence. Good groundwork, research, and quick decisions will not only impress your client, but make selection of goods and ordering materials and equipment easier, save precious time, and reduce costs. Along with organisation, I would list adaptability. The very nature of display work means changes — changes in the space available, budget, deadlines, and many other factors. The ability to cope with these and still keep on course is vital and desirable.

After my humble beginnings in the display world, I was

obliged to serve for two years in the Royal Air Force. Two wasted years as far as I was concerned, as I had long since made my own bed and knew how to brew a cup of tea. There was certainly no outlet for artistic expression in clerical duties at S.H.Q. Afterwards I had a succession of jobs and freelance activities which led to my appointment as senior display man at a delightful, rather old fashioned department store, a stone's throw from Buckingham Palace, whose main claim to fame were the numerous royal crests above the entrance. Members of our royal family often popped in for a brief shopping excursion. The fact that the store specialised in uniforms for all the right schools was the reason it had carried on for so long. However, I continued to gain experience and it was a step nearer the West End stores. The next jump was a major one.

For many years I had admired the displays at Liberty in Regent Street, under the direction of Roy Gentry. His display team were second to none at this time — I refer to the late 50s, early 60s. Suddenly, through a friend who worked there, I had a chance to join that team. The next six years were full of hard work, introductions, projects, and excursions. The prestige of the company washed over me and suddenly I found a new confidence. The very fact of working for Liberty seemed to give me a head start. Friends, who hitherto had taken for granted or ignored the skills or tastes I possessed, suddenly sat up and took notice. If I suggested a colour, or a place for a group of pictures, lo and behold it was done. The magic of a name or label still works and the mark of my years with that wonderful store is with me still. It was there under the critical eye of Roy Gentry that I handled a tremendous variety of merchandise. One day we would be arranging silk rugs from Persia, the next, floral linen luggage from Italy, not to mention the wonderful printed wools, silks, and cottons that were displayed in the fake Tudor galleries. The store was a great attraction for Continental and American visitors who loved the period style of the place.

Above: hessian panels with relief
decoration in fabrics, mosses, and seeds
by the author made a simple but effective
foil for a series of Liberty fabric
displays. This corner window had a
double-sided panel with point drapes on
both sides.
Following pages: a series of Liberty
windows by the author. Thousands of
ice cream cones and wafers act as props
and backgrounds. An economic scheme
with dramatic lighting which caused
much comment.

It was with Liberty that I learned the art of grouping, a skill without which it is impossible to create good displays. Many seemingly empty windows were really full with a mass of goods. At Christmas time, in particular, I can remember counting 360 items in a display of mixed gifts ranging through glass, china, records, jewellery, leather goods and much more, yet the display was easy to look at and uncrowded.

During my stay I had the privilege of working with many well known people — photographers such as Norman Parkinson, Terrence Donovan, and Richard Avedon. Well known designers and artists were featured. I worked for Robert Carrier on photograph sessions arranging dishes on pine dressers for a colour supplement feature. We were loaned out to drape Liberty fabrics on live models for top magazines, exhibitions, and manufacturers' promotions. There were showcases to dress in London hotels and flowers to arrange for receptions. All these activities, added to the studio work carried out high up on the rooftops above Regent Street, where we created props, made for a busy and productive time. This wealth and variety of work gave me a fund of experience so much needed for my next position.

The jump from actually creating displays to teaching people how to do it from scratch, was a big one. It is one thing to know, another to teach what you know. When I started at The London Institute (CDT) in Charing Cross Road, I was not really prepared for the sudden change from physical to mental activity. I was part of a team teaching students on a two year display course. For the first year I can remember feeling exhausted at the end of each session, wondering whether the fountain of ideas, talk, and information would dry up. Now some twenty years later, I still feel that same excitement for my students that I felt for myself as a beginner. We cannot always use the past as our inspiration: there are new directions in treatments and new approaches to colour.

Right: the author's work in a series of tableaux at Liberty in the 1960 Cargo of Silks exhibition. Specially sculpted figures set off the fabric drapes. Cut-out maps and brass globe-like structures back up the theme.

Look back through old magazines or such ephemeral items as programmes, posters, or package designs, and you will see not only the stamp of their creators but the style and graphics of their time. There are classic ideas which designers and display men fall back on time and time again but the discerning eye will note the subtle changes whether, for instance, in proportion, pattern, or colour. The subject must be approached with a fresh mind and viewpoint. The danger with any period of teaching is in neglecting to keep one's visual senses stimulated. I have tried hard to prevent this by accepting all manner of commissions.

The last 15 years have taken me to many places, some glamorous, some quite ordinary. I have lectured and demonstrated the length and breadth of the country to thousands of people, the vast majority not in the retail or display field. There is a great need for our expertise by many people: craftsmen who simply want to show and sell what they make; art students involved with their diploma shows who are sadly lacking in technical know-how when it comes to presenting their skills. Beautiful clothes, jewellery, carvings, and graphics are often laid on tables or pinned to panels in the most basic manner. Charity organisers and teachers working on themes or projects are often confronted with very small areas in which to cram a whole form's contribution. Worse still is the huge barn, hall, or community centre which has to be filled seemingly with a handful of merchandise or exhibits. In all these examples, and in many more, a knowledge and understanding of presentation skills and techniques is invaluable. Throughout this book the reader will find ideas which can be adapted in some way to suit another venue or need.

Returning to my own particular sphere, I have been very much involved with the teaching and demonstration of display techniques, not only to students embarking on a career in the merchandising field, but to various fringe groups eager to utilise the potential which good presentation can give them. Notable among these were my visits to some of thousands of clubs belonging to The National Association of Floral Arrangement Societies (NAFAS). This is a huge ever growing movement with an international section. Their national shows and all their other activities contain work of the highest standards. Talking and working with many of these clubs brought home to me how much we can learn from others and how many of our skills and basic rules are shared. We can never afford to relax in our quest for new ideas, techniques, or trends. We can tour an exhibition, attend a show or film, or just visit a friend's house to find ideas, some staring us in the face, others hidden away and waiting to be used. It is the searching for and working out of these ideas that puts the spice into our job.

Above: real or false? The author's solution for the Jetmaster factory entrance hall brings a dash of humour to an industrial interior. Fake: dog, view, painting, plant, and frame. Real: Jetmaster fire, basket, and staircase.

The rewards can be great or small. Sometimes a happy accident of colours and textures blending or clashing, whichever may suit the occasion, will look perfect. Another time we may have laboured long and arduously over our sketches, worked into the night, finishing our presentation with meticulous attention to detail only to find the end result below our expectations. These are the rules of the game, like a first night in the theatre we can never be sure of results.

I once had the privilege of working with a display legend, Annie Baumel, who had captured Paris for years with her amazing displays for Hermes in the Fauborg St. Honoré. She was visiting London for a specially organised competition and I was given to her as a willing slave. Filling a huge window area with twigs she proceeded to throw silk scarves, gloves of the finest suede, and a spattering of other small accessories very casually onto them; with a few deft touches she perfected the groupings. The dressing took no more than twenty minutes, the arranging of the twigs, four hours. After stretching soft grey net across the entire display, she stepped back, turned on three spotlights, and lo and behold the entire display sprang to life. Gone were the stark twigs and dressmaker's net. In front of me were scarves and gloves glowing with rich patterns and textures against the almost black tracery of twigs — a perfect foil for the luxury of the merchandise. The grey net in its turn had softened the whole effect, transforming everything into a misty tableau, very French, very elegant. I stood amazed at the speed and disarming simplicity that had effected this. I was seventeen at the time and, before I could speak, Annie Baumel, in very broken English, said, 'It is so easy to torture things in display, but very difficult to be natural.'

3: Basic Concepts

Ideas

Where do our ideas come from? A simple question that really has no simple answer. Show three people the same picture or let them flick through a magazine and the response of each will be completely different.

We all take in a vast amount of visual material every day. Posters, television, books, views, people — we cannot possibly store all this up for future use, so we sort out the mass mentally and filter the images or ideas that have had the most impact on us. This process relies on a sort of mental shorthand. The trained display person does this automatically: we store our ideas away at the ready for instant use when the need arises. Of the many areas of display work, the skill of formulating and searching for ideas and inspiration has been the most difficult for me to teach. A person has it or has not, and it can be a long and arduous task to make the seed germinate.

Generally when asked by students how to go about the business of collecting ideas I suggest the setting up of folders, files, or boxes, to store cuttings, photographs, magazine pages, calendars, and cards — in fact anything which contains the germ of an idea. Display can be found almost anywhere. For instance, I can be inspired by looking at the way the woman sitting opposite me in the train has put her ensemble together. Likewise ideas can emerge from or even a form of beauty be seen in a junk yard or factory. In magazines it may be the way a certain type of face is used, an abstracted form, pictures from a famous photographer, or simply a fashion model's make-up or hair styling. Ideas for the classroom, for parties, or for filling rainy afternoons often spring from sorting through such folders.

There are certain display links with items like masks, headdresses, stage decor, and costume, and with lighting schemes and screen and panel treatments in interiors. These make wonderful reference sources. Organise sections relating to colour, seasons, Christmas, children, black & white, Victor-

Preceding page: physical balance and visual balance. The left hand column shows a symmetrical arrangement. The central column shows an imbalance when the focal area—triangle, lamp, and circle—is not well placed. The right hand column shows a balanced effect.

iana, folk art, symbols and motifs, entertainment, surprise ideas, and so on. Subdivide as your collection grows. It is amazing how many exciting and colourful images go out with the refuse, so keep a folder with you all the time and see how quickly you build up an interesting pool of ideas. Don't search specifically for pictures that look like displays but cast your net wider. Be aware of what is going on in all the arts, even if it is an event or exhibition that you are not remotely interested in — you can always sort out at frequent intervals and scrap the pages that you feel will not be of use. Look at creative work around you and analyse the permutations that are being worked on tried and tested themes. Figure out why some work and others look stale.

Being a compulsive shopper and supply source hound myself, I constantly update a somewhat bulging black folio that I keep for companies and individuals who supply our trade, for names of prop makers, for hire firms, and for manufacturers of felt, fabric papers, and so on. This, over a period, is a wonderful time-saver and once again needs to be updated and checked at regular intervals.

When discussing ideas with students, there does seem to be a definite feeling that they must try to be original at all costs. This continual striving after the new and unusual can sometimes lead to disaster. If we take a critical look at the last few decades in design and decoration, we will find quite a few innovators and individuals who have made their mark with an original contribution. These are few, however, compared to the thousands who have copied and adapted the old. Visual clichés abound in the graphic arts and the same applies to display. Time and again we use symbols, props, and copy giving it a fresh twist by attacking the idea from a new and different angle. More often than not, distance lends enchantment and even as I write, the London stores seem to be hooked on a sixties theme with the boutiques of Covent Garden and

Following page: one of the author's first displays in 1951. Notice the almost symmetrical arrangement of models and prop. The eyes, however, are an idea that we see time and again as symbol or motif.

Left: ideas can also bring a touch of humour, here seen in a Bond Street optician's windows in 1965. We could work many variations on such a theme. *Right:* these cartoon-like characters of card and paper all sport real spectacles. *Top:* paper carol singers dressed in fabric all feature glasses from the optician's ranges.

Mayfair awash with splashy prints bright colours and op art. Next season, next year, this look will probably go back into mothballs to be revamped at some future time.

Here are just a few schemes that pop up every year in one guise or another, which always work, given fresh treatment and sympathetic merchandise with good handling and grouping.

An all white display. White on white on white sounds boring but with spotlights and merchandise of varied textures — leather, wool, ceramics, glass — is eye-catching. Groups of white gift-wrapped presents or a collection of clothes on models in white have the same effect. Do not be tempted to dot colour here and there, you will kill the effect. This monochrome technique works well with practically any colours and merchandise. It may seem obvious but it always has impact.

Black and white together can also look striking. Designers and decorators have used it over and over again to great effect — one only has to cast the mind back to the Ascot scene in My Fair Lady. Beaton's triumphant costumes were breathtaking. Black and white merchandise, perhaps with silver or grey added, can be both dramatic and subtle. If a colour is added, be restrained and do not always settle for the obvious red carnation, scarf, or hat. Use instead, perhaps, a jewel colour revealed as a lining or the sparkle of gold, silver, or crystal.

Other schemes that seem to slip in and out of fashion depend on strong contrasts: black and orange, black and yellow, or bold stripes in assorted widths. The reverse is also sure fire success: muted shades, heather colours, bronzes, browns, taupe, grey greens — all feature in first class displays every year as the leaves fall.

Real leaves can be a wonderful foil in all sorts of merchandise, their superb colours left natural or sprayed to suit your

Right:
Above: A well balanced student display using unrelated items. Stationery, fabric, a clock, and other items are given interest by the bows on sticks and the line of plastic ducks.
Below: bows on delicate white painted twigs. The white speckled urn and background intensify the scarlet of the dresses and bows.

scheme. Dried leaves freshly gathered from the garden, countryside, or park can be used in so many ways. Try lightly covering a gauze or net backcloth with them — a dab of glue secures each one and lo and behold a fantastic backdrop or hanging can make your window or showcase glow with colour.

Do not forget basic materials like lightweight blocks or bricks — wall type structures or abstract constructions can be built by stacking and then secured by a nail or two. Gear the shape and form of your construction or screen to accept easily the type of merchandise you are showing.

If a poster or large graphic panel is available to co-ordinate with your display, this is often a good focal point. It can be mounted or framed either in a simple or elaborate way as suits your theme. Stained wood, simple rough hewn timber, or decorative gilt frames can be brought into play to turn the poster into an integral part of the window.

I list here, purely for fun, many more of the well worn display themes that can and do crop up continually.

Dressmaker's dummies in all guises
Eyes, large and small
Giant sweets (in fact giant anything)
Kitchen dressers
The drawn back curtain
Cherubs
Photographic blow ups
Maps
Sign posts

Artist's palettes
Topiary
Branches and twigs
Silhouettes
Dressing room mirrors
Lips
Bows
Bouquets of roses
Masks
Clowns
Screens

Right: A group of students based their work on the style of the painter Seurat. Thousands of tiny specks of colour built up the background and figure. China was arranged in the foreground. There are many artists whose style can be copied and used with a suitable merchandise.

Anyone working over a period in display work will not only recognise all these, but be able to add their own familiar favourites. Ideas emerge and flow like a river from its source but don't forget that you have to keep feeding the supply.

Pattern

As with all elements of the visual arts, patterns can date us. The discerning eye in the world of fashion, graphics, or advertising, can date a picture by just looking at the patterns used in the decor or clothing. This means that we must be in touch with trends or else consciously use a dated effect to gain period mood and atmosphere. There are obvious examples such as Regency stripes, check ginghams, flowery chintzes, and Italian damasks which evoke a mood or feel that can set the tone of a display or interior. Tartans, plaids, spots, spatter, and geometric designs are all used over and over again by artists and designers in many fields.

Although many of the classic rules for using pattern have been turned upside down in the last ten years, certain basics do still apply. Vertical patterns or stripes will give height and elegance. Horizontal lines or borders will give an appearance of breadth. Designs or patterns that have a strong diagonal content will add impact. Instability or the image of imbalance can give exhibits or displays an excitement and interest. Rhythmic patterns of flowing curves or entwining plants can often add grace and appeal to boring or plain items. We can clash patterns as we do with colour: truly exciting effects can be achieved by mixing bold stripes, zig-zags, spots, and checks. Fashion and interior decoration magazines use these techniques constantly — study them and take your ideas into the three-dimensional.

We must remember that we use pattern itself almost unconsciously all the time. Groups of objects, jewellery, or shoes arranged on a plain table or floor make patterns themselves. Lighting can cast shadows that decorate a whole wall area. The leaves of plants silhouetted against a screen or panel will add a strong pattern element to an otherwise plain display. These extra shapes can prove a design bonus but must be watched as too much conflicting pattern, too many interesting shapes, can cause conflict and spoil a well balanced arrangement or scheme.

Right: pattern plays an important part in this Liberty window: used here with the panels as a background, and with the help of a column and screen which add depth and focus our interest on the figures. The model standing in the foreground reinforces the effect by casting her eyes onto the group.

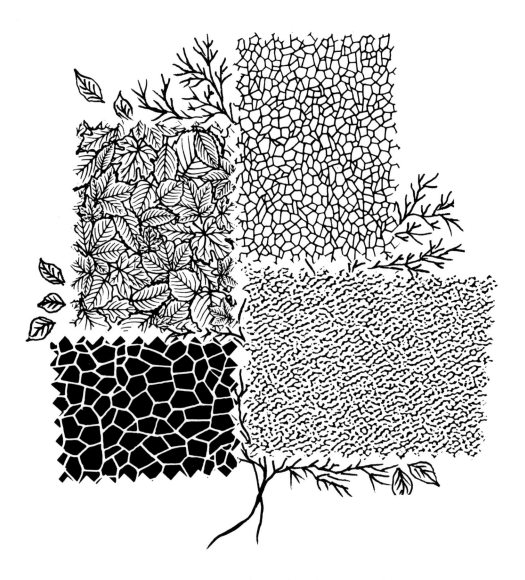

Above: These four patterns have a natural feel, enhanced by the crazy paving, textures, and leaf motifs. A mood which could be used for a group of fashion items, wallpapers, or fabrics.

Left:

Above: a mixture of classical patterns gives this Sanderson room set a timeless quality. Floor and walls contrast strongly but the overall effect is harmonious. Note use of wallpaper on the marbled column—an easy idea to adapt for use in many display situations.

Below: pattern, shapes, and grouping illustrated in this Liberty scarf display.

Grouping

The ability to arrange or bring together related or unrelated items in an interesting and eye arresting manner is crucial to display.

Items will be chosen for a variety of heights, sizes, textures, or prices. Obvious rules have to be followed like grouping colours and patterns and selecting some items for focal areas. For instance, the designer gown with a sensational back view will have pride of place; likewise a set of suitcases in scarlet leather will be the main feature in a display of black and grey leather goods. A good group often consists of one or two larger or more important items as the focus or core with other smaller or less interesting objects closely overlapping or placed next to them and with a strong feel for the general outline.

Shape and proportion are of prime importance. Sometimes we rely strongly on the triangular grouping method — the arrangement beloved of display people and flower arrangers alike. Other groupings can be attempted long and low. We may opt for diagonal shapes. Smaller groups can be contained within one large group or form a cascade down steps or shelf units. The one great advantage of tight crisp groups is that they can show a greater variety of merchandise whilst leaving space around the design.

Should the design be asymmetric or symmetric? That is the question confronting not only display people but designers, architects, photographers, and in fact anyone who is involved in organising material or people.

The symmetric balance allows for no variation — what we place on one side must have a corresponding item on the other side. This applies to buildings, page layout, and posters, or stage, textile, and wallpaper designs. If we are seeking a good basic classical format or grouping, then a symmetric arrangement is the answer.

Symmetry is ideally suited to the formal, serious venue. An

old master on display in a museum would look all wrong set on the slant and away from the centre of its setting. Likewise a four-tiered wedding cake centrally placed on a buffet table automatically becomes the focus of the whole event.

The very predictability of symmetry can add many visual qualities. For example, an avenue of trees or a formal arrangement of hedges and flower beds gives structure, vistas, and elegance to a garden. The simple pillars and arches of a church or soaring columns and fan vaulting in a cathedral give a great sense of perspective and order as they frame an altar or screen, the picture completed with rich hangings or simple flowers.

What is the connection between this and commercial display? The answer is that the elements are the same. We have our balanced picture: organised space with a focal area. The fact remains, however, that a symmetrical arrangement is very predictable. Once you have seen one half of the design, you have more or less seen the other. In display terms this can sometimes kill off any sense of excitement or spontaneity.

I find that complete newcomers on their first encounters with arrangements of merchandise nine times out of ten will settle for a symmetrical layout. They make their first placement with an object, model, or fabric bang in the middle of the area. This in a stroke divides the display into two halves. The rest follows automatically — it seems a natural way to arrange goods be it a charity bazaar or market stall.

Right! So this symmetric or equal balance is not necessarily the answer, but it is easy if it takes the guesswork out of filling a space. How do I set about the asymmetric or unbalanced grouping? The key here is the word *unbalanced*. In spatial and volume terms it may well be unbalanced but visually it looks right. The oriental designers and artists understand this type of arrangement perfectly.

In our symmetric arrangement the focus of interest is usually dead centre. The moment we move this focal spot to

left or right we start composing a completely different picture, our framework remains the same but the elements within now have to be rearranged in such a manner that we still retain a visual balance. This visual balance can be achieved in a number of ways. For instance, with fridges or freezers, we use the shapes, the squares or rectangles, to form balanced groups, adding interest with graphics or price tickets. With textiles we use rhythmic and linear control to give structure, working with the plasticity and draping qualities of the goods.

Beyond the symmetric or asymmetric, there are two further ways of laying out a display. The repeated group, based, as the titles suggests, on the repetition of a group or series of groups. Most effective where there is space and a long run of display area, this can be used with small goods in series of showcase displays or within departments in stores showing a variety of merchandise. The other type of layout is the all over grid effect, usually achieved by shelves or units. This divides the space into a series of smaller boxes which can vary in size or be modular. In this case we treat each unit separately but pay attention to the finished whole.

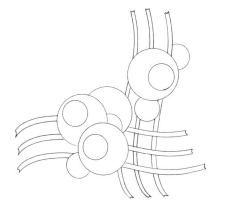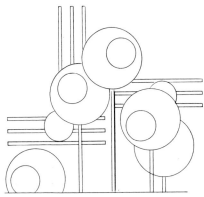

Above: experiment with straight and curved lines, and with shapes and backgrounds to create rhythm or structure.
Left:
Above: Crayonne Input plastic containers in a casual arrangement of toys. Note that the tubs themselves remain the focal point in this publicity photo.
Below: styling shot for Kitchen Devil knife. Note the choice of a subtle, patterned, wooden block. The knife's function is shown by the carefully cut and placed vegetables. The knife holds the composition together—place your finger over it and see the grouping fall apart.

Above: greetings cards are arranged in tightly grouped formations. The satin ribbons add line and focus our eyes on the designs.

Right: grouping of Adel Rootstein figures in her New York showroom demonstrates the success of good placement. Poses and varying heights of figures add drama.

Above: greetings cards by Catherine Brighty, herself an ex display student. The penguins march across the card in repetition—an idea often used with models and merchandise. The second card shows the penguins grouped informally and facing different directions, the overlapping adding depth. Note the balanced arrangement of space, and design within the space. The understanding of this unfilled space is a key to any display grouping.

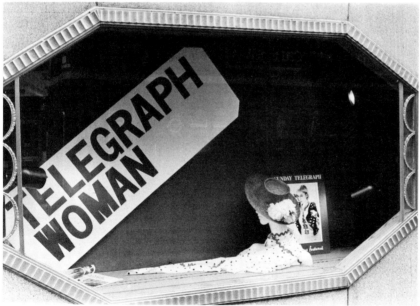

Above: grouping here shown in its simplest form at the Royal Academy Horses of San Marco exhibition. Everything is grouped at eye level and the dark background and concentrated lighting reinforce the dramatic effect.

A showcase display for a newspaper uses grouping effectively. We are not selling merchandise but a name and a page.

Window Shapes and Sizes

Windows, like shops themselves, vary enormously in shape and size. Suffice it to say that if I included diagrams and visuals to help the reader with a hundred varying window sizes, your own problem area would not be amongst them. We have therefore to speak in general terms, and whilst these may not deal specifically with your personal display areas, common sense will point out your best plan of attack.

A lot depends, when we refer to the ideal window size, on what we are selling. The jeweller, the shoe shop, a store setting up a linen display — all have different needs. It is not only size but depth, ease of entry, suspension points, or a grid. If you add to these the height of the floor from pavement or sidewalk level, lighting fittings, and so on the variables are endless. The best plan is to look around at a variety of shops selling within the same area of merchandise as yourself.

In most cases we are stuck with a shopfront, but it is surprising how many retailers have a hand in the design of their shops and ignore the display area. Too late they discover no real facilities and also no attractive areas left for exciting displays.

Let us look at a few typical difficult shapes we might own or encounter.

The tall window Usually found in older premises. The focal points or interest areas can only be brought down by focusing attention at eye level. We can do this in several ways. We can select a dark background and use strong spotlighting on our low groupings of stock in order to lose the height and space. Alternatively we can use prosceniums or frameworks to cut down our picture — pelmets and curtains or painted out areas of glass can help with this.

Wide windows Long windows with no dividing panels or partitions can appear rather bleak and empty, especially if merchandise is on the small side. Again, curtains at the side can look attractive and bring the shop decor into the display. These can be swept back or swagged to suit your style. Panels or fake window frames can be used to divide the glass into smaller sections. Colour and lighting can break up what may otherwise be a long boring stretch of display area. Verticals in the form of panels, screens, blocks, curtains, or graphics can break the horizontal line.

Shallow windows There is little that can be done as depth is an important factor in many compositions. Use the back wall to full advantage by mounting flat panels on it to take merchandise, by fixing narrow shelf units to it, or by choosing dark colours which make the background recede. Spotlight your merchandise from overhead rather than the side or floor. These can all give a feeling of depth.

Deep windows Here our problems are best solved by clever use of false backgrounds — treat the display rather like a stage set. Use its depth but keep your merchandise well forward as it can get swallowed up in the space. Blinds, screens, and panels dropped from the ceiling all cut up the space. Lighting on the merchandise from the sides helps focus attention towards the front of the display area. Try to ignore the back wall, do not light it or feature it any more than you have to. In the case of furniture displays or room settings, of course, the depth will be a great help to you.

Island windows These can vary in shape and give us the awkward prospect of arranging merchandise, models, and props to be viewed from four angles. All round showcases used to be very popular in arcades and some stores still possess them. In most cases the situation is not as bad as it seems. A narrow panel can slip down in the centre of the display, you then dress this from the front and back, and as it is narrow, the panel does not affect side views. Blinds or screens can be used to give an impression of a background. Try putting models back to back in fashion groupings or stack up merchandise with a spiralling line of interest running through your group. An example could be found in a pile of luggage stacked up case upon case using the smaller sizes at the top — a wide range of items could be shown on the cases coming out of them or on the floor of the display. Depending on the size of the display, a model or two in travelling gear or holiday clothes could be included.

This OXFAM shop, like many charity shops, has a constantly changing range of goods to show. The window area here has an ideal solution. A simple wooden structure and ceiling with glass shelves and suspension facilities giving a great deal of flexibility.

Preparation

Display, like so many other activities, relies on a great deal of planning and preparation.

Opinions vary on how we visualise our designs. Certainly students go through the process of learning how to put their ideas and schemes onto paper. The ability to draw or sketch is an asset but not a prerequisite of the budding display person. I work on the premise that I relate my preparatory visual submissions to the assignment. Detailed drawings, lists of material, and costings may be needed if the job in hand is complex or on a contract basis. For smaller jobs and commissions carried out directly with the buyer or designer, roughs and samples of colours and materials will suffice along with a verbal description. On some occasions the finished display may be rather different from the original conception, as new ideas strike the imagination, but this uncertainty is part of the job's attraction.

Once the specifications are agreed and the date for the display arrives, work begins. A box of tools and equipment can be brought on the assignment as listed below.

Staple gun or tacker, a lightweight model makes the job easier
Staples and Staple Remover
Pins, both normal steel pins and small pins for fine work
Hammer, size depends on the type of work you are doing
Pliers and Pincers
Panel pins and a selection of nails
A variety of screws and screw hooks
Nylon thread for suspension and securing
Cotton, black and white, for suspending lightweight items
Wire, a reel of fine florists' wire is ideal
Adhesives, tubes of general purpose and spray adhesive
Double sided tape and masking tape
Pencil
Measuring tape
Scissors
Small stiff brush or flick
Duster or pack of paper cloths

Cutting knife
Elastic bands
A bottle of glass cleaning fluid

The above are all essential to me, but your list will vary to suit your needs. Other items might include:
A camera, useful for reference later on if job is one of a series
Car vacuum cleaner, for awkward spaces or odd corners
Pegs, useful for holding fabrics or fashions without using pins
Bulldog clips, for use as above
Small saw
Tippex, for touching in chips or scratches
Felt pens, for use as above

Areas to be used for the display must be cleared and painted or covered in readiness for the merchandise to be featured. Materials like glass, carpet, wood, or metal should be spotless and ready before work commences and the window should be sparkling clear. Cleanliness and the removal of old display rubbish like staples, pins, and scraps of previous covering materials are very important.

The next stage is to see that all fixtures, units, or cylinders are ready for use and that tickets, showcards, panels, and props are prepared. Stock or merchandise should be selected and standing by before the artistic work begins.

If the display areas are large or a series of displays is to be executed, then all this preparation is very time consuming and allowances for it must be made in time schedules and budgets. Some stores change their displays at night or at weekends to ease this problem.

Just as preparation is essential to a good display, so, too, work stands or falls by the way it is executed and finished off. Crooked pictures on a wall, dusty bottles, misty mirrors, lampshades or wigs askew, textiles that do not hang straight, or scarves unpressed — all these details need constant vigilance. We are the last, as it were, to leave the stage before curtain up and we should leave a perfect setting.

4: Merchandise

It is impossible to give guidelines for every kind of stock but I list here some general points and ideas which will help with a wide range of merchandise and which should provide inspiration for the display of many other goods.

I would like to open this chapter by dealing with merchandise manipulation. When we talk of manipulating merchandise we refer to items or garments that have no rigid construction or shape, this naturally includes all textiles. The first thing to bear in mind, when attempting to display flexible or soft goods, is that we can, to some extent, mould or shape them into our scheme. When working with hard goods we know that a suitcase or lamp cannot be anything other than a suitcase and a table lamp. Items such as sweaters, duvets, baby clothes, towels, and blankets can all be treated in many differing ways. In other words, the handling can enhance and help the display and become part of its overall design.

One major rule that I try to follow is never to torture or contort merchandise. All too often we observe pleating, ruching, overpinning, or suspension that has distorted garments and fabrics alike. Merchandise of good quality needs minimal handling — let it speak for itself. We should never lose sight of our aim: to sell the items we are displaying.

Preceding page: a small group of perfumery can be stretched visually, in this case, by the specially made dress which echoes the mood of the Giorgio perfume itself. Note that the figure's gaze is directed at the copy panel.

Furnishing Fabrics

All fabrics created for the home and interior decoration market have one thing in common. They are designed specifically to be used and viewed as part of a scheme, whether domestic or contract. They are intended to be made into curtains, blinds, wall coverings screens, upholstery, or loose covers. Occasionally we might find dramatic interiors using fabrics in an unusual manner, such as swagged and tented ceilings and walls, but these are the exception. With this in mind I feel it is therefore best to approach and handle furnishing textiles in a straightforward manner. All too often we see great swags and drapes of pinned and pleated fabric that has much more connection with the fashion scene than the interiors that the fabrics themselves will inhabit eventually. This does not mean that we cannot go wild from time to time as both fashion and interior magazines do. We are currently seeing a tremendous crossing over of styles and uses for cloth and this is a good thing, but must be kept in check or the novelty and surprise element is soon lost.

I list below the methods most often used for furnishing fabrics.

The straight pleat Fabric is attached to wall, panel, or framework with pins, or staple gun (tacker). Good for soft silky handle fabrics or textures.

Pinch pleat As above, but pleats are left free-standing and this gives more depth to folds. Ideal for textures, small prints, velvets, nets and sheers.

Flat Fabric is pinned or stretched onto panels to give an appearance of a covered wall area. This method is ideal for large prints, checks, or stripes.

Swag or bias drapes The cloth is fixed on the bias of the fabric and the curves produced by this are caught up and tied or attached to give swagged valance or curtain effects. This

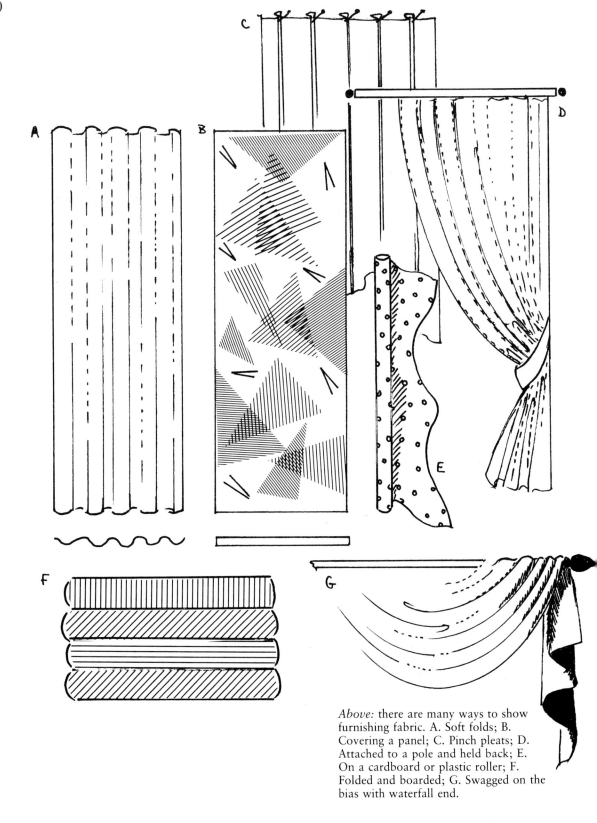

Above: there are many ways to show furnishing fabric. A. Soft folds; B. Covering a panel; C. Pinch pleats; D. Attached to a pole and held back; E. On a cardboard or plastic roller; F. Folded and boarded; G. Swagged on the bias with waterfall end.

form of draping needs care and attention, but beautiful folds and shapes can be achieved. The principles involved can be quite easily understood by studying any book on curtain making.

Display people are currently exploring new methods and treatments of furnishing fabrics and giving new life to an area that has changed little over my career. One of the modern trends is to use poles as the framework or prop and to throw the lengths of fabric over them, sometimes with the cloth caught up and knotted, sometimes hanging freely.

Generally speaking ideas suggest themselves when we first see the ranges of colours or prints to be shown. There may well be matching bed linen, table covers, cushions, lampshades, or photograph frames that co-ordinate or tie in with our scheme. We can use our methods of handling to achieve variety and interesting contrasts such as solid set against sheer, curves cutting across verticals, sculptural folds or handling to throw up the nature of the fabric. Just drop a length of velvet, brocade, satin, or a dralon net onto a carpet and see how each piece falls in its own manner. Use this handle. The actual look and feel of the fabric is telling you something. Don't fight it or try to change it, use it and your task is made that much simpler.

Above: co-ordinated accessories to match the hand blocked chintz in this casual arrangement for the Charles Hammond Shop, a method which works best with high quality merchandise.

Above: display styled for Dorma is carefully composed with the lamp and chair directing attention onto the bed.

Another room set for Dorma shows a simple way of framing the bed. Gauzy white curtains soften and emphasize the boldly checked duvet and pillows. Foreground birds add strong contrast.

Above: this feminine window treatment styled for the Curtain Net Advisory Bureau is easily copied. Soft lace, voile, or net is swagged and caught up with satin bows, the ends falling in tiers.

The fusing of display and a room set with free treatment of fabric and casual placing of the rolls of wallpaper.

Fashion Fabrics

With fashion fabrics, the display person has a seemingly clean canvas to work upon. This in a way is the fabric's attraction and sometimes the display person's undoing. We are creating all the shapes within our display (apart from models, if they are used).

There are so many ways of displaying dress and fashion fabrics but display people rely a great deal on the following methods. Of course variations and new ideas crop up all the time but these classic drapes are the mainstay for most lay-outs.

The flat pleat　As with furnishings the cloth is pinned or stapled to fall as a curtain would hang. Ends can be draped, left loose, or pulled tightly to form rigid pleated areas.

The point drape　Fabrics are suspended by one corner, the rest of the cloth is draped and fashioned into pleats. The results should form a crescent of fabric, narrow or wide according to the width of the fabric. This method looks good in groups of points consisting of contrasting or toning colours and textures.

The bias swag drape　Similar to the point drape but the fabric is bunched or gathered into a loop, or held on a small suspended perch. This affects the way the fabric falls and we get a larger, fuller version of the point drape, with a cascade of fabric and a tail on the end. Very effective and useful with brocades, thick richly textured lamés, lurex weaves, and tweeds.

Bias sculpture　Fabric sculpture as practised some years ago so brilliantly by the Swiss and German schools of display is not used as much now. This is a pity because at its best it can look truly stunning and be used in many varied settings. We do see occasional bursts of this technique in the pages of *Inspiration* and *Das Shauffenster*. Fabric is pleated across the bias, a line diagonal to the warp and weft of the cloth. This is then worked into loops, swags, swirls, and undulating ripples of fabric. The overall shapes created can be a major feature or relate to other items on show. This technique works very well if the fabrics are colour grouped with an exciting range of textures, weaves, and patterns.

Figure and model draping   To drape and create designs with your fabrics on actual models is a very useful, and a most suitable way of displaying them. From the selling viewpoint cloth shown on figures has a great advantage. If one or two prints or colours from a range are featured on models, then almost invariably these will sell out first. More work for the display assistant but also more cash in the cash register. This after all, is the purpose of commercial display — to boost and encourage sales.

Model draping as such is a specialised skill and should not be attempted by the beginner. Restraint and a sympathetic approach to the fabric, coupled with an understanding of style and colour are the qualities needed. It is all too easy to make a perfectly good display mannequin look like a Christmas tree. The fabric itself provides the trigger to your inspiration — go with it and in many instances it will do half the work for you. Let the crepe and silk jersey fall into soft folds as it wants to. Take a firm hand with the taffetas and brocades, they need control to play up their angular handling quality.

If the reader smiles at these references to a lifeless thing such as fabric on its cardboard roll, then he or she needs to watch cloth unfurl from its board or tube and spring to life in the hands of an experienced display person. To attempt fabric draping on figures a clear mental picture is needed of the finished shape and style. This may alter as you proceed but a definite end vision should be borne in mind. Study the fashion magazines for styles that transfer to pinning and avoid complicated tailored garments if you can, these are best left alone if the fabric is to remain our prime reason for draping a figure. We are indeed fortunate that there are so many looks currently

Above and left: period costume and props
were created by students for this studio
exercise. Fabrics in rich shades draped the
figures. Chests, shields, and hangings
were made from foil, hardboard, hessian,
and junk.

Above: this display of Liberty printed
fabric tied up with an exhibition of Pre-
Raphaelite Art at the Tate Gallery.

Above: a figure drape on an abstracted
model forms the focal point of this
group of patterned and plain fabrics.
Note the sweep of the point drapes
balanced by the drapes to the floor.

in vogue that can easily be fashioned from fabric metreage. Kimono and kaftan type garments lend themselves to this type of fabric display, as do all styles that rely on the flow achieved by bias draping.

Figures may well be all that are needed in a display but we are often asked to feature a selection of other shades in a range or wider choice of fabrics. When this happens we usually treat the models as our main focal area and include point drapes or panels covered in fabric as a backup. Fabrics can be shown on rolls or boarded and stacked. The important thing to remember is that the figures are an integral part of the scheme, not an additional item surrounded by other fabrics.

Above: a standing figure and a kneeling one adorned with vivid paper flowers are the only props in this student display of chiffons.
Right: when teaching or demonstrating, speed is essential. This island display by the author was thrown together for a class in less than ten minutes. The fabrics themselves and their handle were featured, rather than a definite fashion or dress design.

Fashion Dressing

Fashion is the hardest type of merchandise about which to be objective, since its world is ever changing. The fashion trade itself has altered almost beyond recognition in a couple of decades. The disappearance of a rigid code of fashion dictated by the top designers in Paris, Rome, London, and New York, however, has made our job easier. We can arrange our displays to suit the image of the company being presented. Our malls and high streets reflect this with a wide range of specialist boutiques and shops. These each have a clearly defined market strategy aiming at a particular age group or type of shopper. Similarly, a department store can, with its shop within shop concessions, have a much wider merchandising spectrum.

Our role, therefore, is to present whatever it is we are promoting in a suitable manner that will attract the specific section of the public who form the potential market. These will, we hope, respond to our selection, type of dressing, and co-ordination. Some will even end up buying an entire look. The fusion of clothes, accessories, and current fashion look or story is very much in the hands of the co-ordinator or display person.

I list here several methods of dressing for female fashion, some classic, some recent additions to our repertoire. An important point to remember is that after the clothes have been displayed, they have to be sold, so take every possible care to handle them gently.

Models   Clothes are really at their best on good figures, well grouped and accessorised. Remember to use as few pins as possible and use small special pins on silk and lingerie. Pegs and bulldog clips can often be used to clasp fabrics together. Have plenty of clean white tissue ready to fold in with flimsy garments, for padding, or simply to lay delicate items on. To achieve a feeling of movement, hems can be wired with a fine wire into the hem, but use this technique sparingly.

Above: a student exercise shows how to dramatise a pair of figures. Pleated paper fans sprayed and edged in black frame the group.

Preceding pages: specially designed
models by Adel Rootstein for the Fortuny
exhibition at Liberty. The proportions
and poses are perfect for the Italian
designers' creations. Fortuny fabrics in
their dark but glowing colours and
patterns completed the many tableaux.
Above: elegant display from Jaeger. The
formal arrangement, almost symmetric in
its balance, is perfect for the groups of
dogs and figures. The screens with their
art deco designs complement the
aristocratic poses of the mannequins.

Above: arresting display of young fashion
at Selfridges in Oxford. The props are
simple but the stiffened fabric, frozen in
its folds, adds drama and movement.
The lighting and placing of the models is
pure theatre.

Hangers A useful way with casual clothes or sports gear. Several garments can be shown one over another. A terrific way to fill an area and achieve height in your groupings economically.

Panels Casual and sports clothing looks good pinned or hung on panels. Backgrounds can harmonize or contrast. Ideal in departmental situations. Showcases with little depth can be treated in this way. Items can be pinned on formally or flow casually over the surface.

Poles Suspended and fixed poles in wood or metal, make not only an interesting design element in a display but can carry clothing as well. Whether folded or flat, sweaters, shirts, and scarves can all look effective arranged over poles.

Platform Floor or platform handling can be interesting particularly with raised floors or sloping panel floors. It looks very easy just laying groups of fashion items on the floor but in fact the simpler the effect in all fashion handling, the more skill is needed.

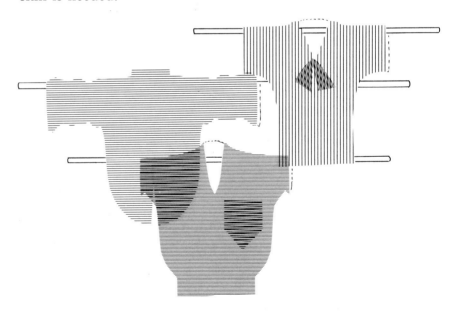

Above: separates can be shown on poles quite easily. Thick knits and simple shapes look their best shown this way.

Above: a student's solution to the
problem of giving some movement to
two rather static figures wearing sports
gear. The placing of the wooden strips
diagonally crossing in the foreground and
behind the models also adds depth.

The traditional methods of handling tailored or formal men's clothing still apply in some situations. Half busts without heads are the usual standby for tailors and shops specializing in such clothes. The bespoke or made to measure tailor's window can still be found in Saville Row and many other places in London. Cloth is usually shown folded on boards alongside fairly basic items such as waistcoats, shoes, ties, and shirts. The correct dressing of such displays is an art in itself, as are the shirt makers' displays in Jermyn Street and the City. Bolts of shirtings are pinched, ruched, and puffed up to look like a row of billows on the ocean. The whole effect is of quality and a tradition which has gone on for ages. If you are dealing with such merchandise you are wise to show it in this age old manner. Your stock and client must be your guide as to handling, colour, and props.

Handling of men's clothing relies on much the same techniques as women's wear. It is however true to say, that greater changes have taken place in men's clothes, than on the women's side. Fashion now does apply to both sexes and a huge proportion of the menswear industry depends on this aspect. The current look or trend is all important when selling to the young male. It is not enough to present a garment any more — a concept or total fashion story are what make the media and the buying public interested. Fix your sights on the type of male your display is aimed at and dress it accordingly.

Co-ordinating your whole display can prove difficult if you have several ranges to show in one area. Remember colours can separate visually. For example the combination of a black and tan group alongside a blue and beige next to grey and navy will blend into a harmonious whole, yet groups will have their own identity. Accessories are every bit as important as in the women's sector and always add that much needed contrast and interest. The contrast of leather belts, suede,

Right: traditional Christmas garlands and pulled back curtains frame this Jermyn Street display of high quality menswear. Shirts, ties, and accessories are shown with boxes tied with ribbons, reinforcing the name Hawes and Curtis.

Above: this interior of a Next for Men shop shows how shopfitting and display can go hand in hand. The windows have pole screens, and every inch of space is used to full advantage.

Right: wooden structures give a strong diagonal emphasis in this John Lewis display. Models are grouped and floor panels define the merchandise area. Poles carry a range of sweaters and shirts. These same structures were later used for carpet and rug displays.

metal, and other textures against plain cloth or tweeds always adds to the finished dressing. From time to time we get the opportunity to add a few small related items. Clichés they may be to us, but still new to the onlooker. In a window showing suits we may add a folded newspaper with a briefcase, an interesting magazine, walking sticks, a scarlet carnation in a grey lapel, stationery items, spectacles, binoculars. With leisurewear we may show sports items or equipment, likewise workwear or jeans could feature tools or oil cans. All these have been used over the years but if used well still look right and help give depth and mood.

Scarves

A scarf can soften a display of rectangular or hard shapes or bring pattern and vibrant colour to dull groups of merchandise.

We have to think of scarves, shawls, throws, quilts, or literally any square or rectangle as a piece of fabric. The same handling techniques apply but size, scale, and setting have to vary.

The bias or diagonal of the weave is brought into play by starting the drapes from the corner. In this manner the drape and sculptural qualities of the item can be used fully. Even flexible rugs and carpets such as silk Persians can be treated in this way. The starting corner of the scarf can be suspended or fixed to a prop, cascades of scarves can be created by attaching a number of them to one point; or they can be fixed to items of furniture, chests of drawers, hat stands, grandfather clock, or even to small decorative trees and dried flower arrangements.

Above: a masterly handling of scarves by Selfridges in Oxford.

If we are dealing with scarves that have large or intricate designs printed on them, then we can treat them as flat areas and feature the designs as we would pictures or record sleeves.

A handful of scarves can be transformed from nothing into beautifully draped displays. They can be ruched, pinned, suspended, pulled, stretched, sculpted, folded or just shown flat. But we must always remember that we are shaping and filling whole areas with our various handling methods. The individual items, though interesting and well displayed in themselves, must form part of a larger or greater design. It can often be a mistake to arrange too many interesting and intricately displayed items in one display. The overall effect is confusing and we miss the odd area of breathing space, the plain to show off the pattern, the foliage to flatter the flower so to speak. It is vital to consider the completed shape of our group as we progress. With all fabrics, fashions, indeed any pliable merchandise that can be manipulated to change its form, we must constantly check on the shapes we are creating. Many beginners fail to do this and their displays suffer as a result.

Left: a unit display at John Lewis with well balanced grouping and point draping of scarves. Note the flow, and strategically placed stars. An ideal method to show quite a lot of stock—especially useful at Christmas.

Cosmetics & Perfume

This is a very important and profitable sector of merchandising. A visit to any large department store or shopping area will give you some idea in terms of space, siting and staffing, of how important it is. All the major companies in this field are competitive in the marketing and presentation of their products. Display and advertising are vital factors and companies neglect them at their peril.

The female public, especially the younger shopper, is remarkably fickle and new product names come and go with amazing rapidity. Most houses adopt a policy and a display style that fits their image. Some rely on stressing the scientific, medical, no nonsense aspects of their product, others make much of fashion, youth, and sex. On the side of the cosmetic market geared towards men, we find exactly the same situation. The appeal is varied and aimed at the sporty, business, romantic, or rugged man. The permutations are endless but an image is what we are selling and it is vital to remember this. In no other marketing or advertising area is this fact so important.

The actual dummy or fake jars and bottles that most manufacturers supply are a delight to look at and arrange. Grouping is easy and quite straightforward — we can use small against tall, round against square to achieve contrast. Point of sale material is quite often supplied and items such as showcards, base units, and panels in acrylic wood or brass usually carry the manufacturer's or product name. Cut-out letters can give interest to the other items on show.

Perfumery and cosmetics are at their best in smaller windows or showcases where we can ring the changes with backgrounds and bases. A variety of fabrics and coverings can be used and seasonal promotions can be given fresh treatments with colour and accessories. At Christmas, especially, when people are window shopping in earnest, groupings can be made up of a mixture of manufacturers' products.

Right: this publicity shot for Lagerfeld, ties the masculine image and the product firmly together in the eye and the mind.

I personally feel it is a great mistake to play on the satins, frills, flowers, and lacy backgrounds all the time. The shopping public are so used to this treatment that it becomes a visual cliché, part of the wallpaper so to speak. On occasions let the gleaming glass flacons and faceted crystal bottles shine and sparkle against contrast or surprise backdrops such as dark brown peat or sheets of rusting oxidized metal. Window cleaner's scrim or raw jute used for sacks make a great background for perfume displays. If the scent is young in mood do not be afraid of using colour: spatter or dribble primary colours onto sheets of perspex or board. Fabrics can be treated in a similar fashion, tie dyed or sprayed and speckled with dyes or bleach. You can achieve really exciting effects quite easily with some plain calico or hessian and an empty studio for an hour or so. Above all do not get into a rut, ruched satin and velvet bows can look fabulous but not all the time.

It is also important not to get too carried away with the trimmings. A handful or two of sand and a group of pebbles or a shell with a summer fragrance. An old gnarled piece of driftwood and some moss with a musky cologne might be just right. Large photographic blow ups of ocean or forest respectively probably would just confuse and add nothing but expense. Pay attention to good dramatic lighting. If possible one or two spots trained on a bottle or group can bring a display to life. Keep it simple and let your products shine through.

Right: one of a series of Gene Moore's Tiffany displays with a carnival theme. Painted backdrops and atmospheric figures by Elliot Arkin. Note the footlights and the placing of the string of pearls—the only item of jewelry.
Overleaf: two displays by Gene Moore at Tiffany.
Valentine display—two linked neon hearts illuminate the heart-shaped enamel boxes. Hearts by John Tanaka.
Real butterflies and a butterfly brooch are poised on a simple wire grid. Lit from behind, this makes the most of a very simple idea.

Books

Bookshops usually have the same problems that befall jewellers and shoe shops. People want to see a good range of stock on display or they will not come in. Specialist bookshops or some of the more sophisticated ones can, and do, devote whole windows to one title, with, perhaps, an author signing session. Many bookshops cannot afford, or just would not dare to devote their windows to such a limited range of stock, so we end up with a real mish mash of titles, sizes, and colours thrown or stacked together. People who love and frequent bookshops as I do myself will not be put off by this. In some ways it gives us the sense of discovery and interest we might experience when peering into a rather messy antique or junk shop. It does not, however, sit happily alongside many other high street retailers and can look downright shabby.

The bookshop with its mass of ever changing subjects and titles, point of sale material, posters and back up campaigns, has a lot going for it. A grand slam display of a best-seller, or a window devoted to a few television hit serials can really attract attention. Subjects can be chosen for special focus such as, health, tourism, gardens, theatre and cinema, children, retirement, or antiques. All these give you the chance to fill your display with a mood and interest, helped by simple props such as plants, an antique table or chair, a doll's house or deck chair, a bunch of corn, or a period costume.

As to the actual handling, the books themselves will dictate this to you. Thin paperbacks or laminated cover books cannot be stood up easily. If you have thirty copies of a popular novel you can stack or fix them to panels in repeating patterns. Nylon thread can be tied round books stopping them opening. Pins should never pierce a book except on special occasions such as a book fair or launch where people would have access and try to pull them off your display. Above all remember that books in the main are exciting and even seemingly dull books can be enlivened and given impact by the right treatment and visual linking with other areas. Dictionaries, for example, might be tied in with word games, ready reckoners with an abacus, and educational text books with board and chalk.

Record and Cassettes

Records, or rather record sleeves, because that is what we are showing, have the benefit of being square and all one size. We are dealing with pictures really, and pictures that are based on a module. Just play with a few record sleeves for a minute or two, you will find that they can be laid out flat like floor tiles, wall mounted with gaps between, pinned up, or suspended in any way you choose. They can be pinned or fixed to make cubes or even curved into sculptural shapes on panels. I like to see record sleeves suspended — this gives a light airy look and features the sleeves well, especially if spotlit. Two pins pushed in to the ridge at the top of the sleeve makes this easy, just thread your cotton through and suspend on the loop.

The introduction of panels, straight or set at angles, can help us with composition and stop the display from looking bitty. This is a real danger with both record and book display. Permanent fixtures or racks can be installed to take tapes or records — these are useful if you do not have an area devoted to pure display. Custom built or stock merchandising units can make for an attractive dual purpose area. Cassettes and compact discs by nature of their size, present different problems but similar layouts are possible — panels and platforms can give much needed height. Stacking or building bricks can look interesting. Small double sided tabs can fix the cassette cases or discs onto many surfaces.

Once again moods and themes can be introduced. A colour scheme does wonders — choose all red, black, and white sleeves or green, turquoise, and blue. You will be amazed at the impact a simple trick like choosing for colour can give to an otherwise multicolour display. It also, as a bonus, gives you a very mixed and catholic selection. Opera, broadway shows, and jazz all sit beside each other by virtue of their sleeve colour. Alternatively the display can be devoted to a particular theme such as ballet, folk music, a composer, or the spoken word.

Stationery

If I could choose any merchandise in the book to show a student what it is possible to achieve by good grouping, then I would have no hesitation in choosing from the stationery section. We have everything going for us: a variety of attractive colours, interesting shapes, boxes, cards, the flexibility of wrapping paper sheets. Add all these together and you will see my point, whether you arrange your groups on panels or on shelves.

Here are several directions and themes which can give a lift to a variety of display areas. Try if possible to get some impact into the display by complementing your colour and type of merchandise. This can be done by background colour, texture, or mood.

Business stationery This can be as plain and boring as manilla envelopes, typing paper, and paper clips. Why not try a chalk stripe fabric panel or a graph-like checked paper or cotton floor insert. Plain slabs of colour can be brought in with a scarlet in-tray or filing cabinet. Try to stress the formal nature of your theme by regimented dressing, straight rows of pens, pads, pencils, stacks of files, trays, and baskets. You will be surprised how the effect grows the more you add. Slatted blinds or plain fabric blinds work well with such groupings.

General stationery Everyday items like pads, cards, envelopes, and boxed sets are just asking to be grouped to colour. A series of small groups set on different level platforms or shelves can include related accessories such as diaries, books, calendars, and in fact anything that will link with your group. If the store sells gift wrapping items, the natural thing to do is to wrap a few attractive boxes, decorate with ribbons, and at once your colour theme is enhanced. The boxes can serve the dual purpose of displaying a range of papers and giving you added height and placements within your groups.

Fashion stationery   A very exciting and attractive section of the trade. Each year brings us yet more vibrant colours and eye catching ideas. Why not take your theme from your stock if a certain colour or motif predominates, use it. Vivid colours and clashing patterns, tropical flowers, cartoon images, romantic pastels — all of these are begging for the full treatment. Net is a cheap material and can be used effectively, it is light and can be obtained in many colours. Felt covered boards in jewel colours can be useful for example when displaying arrangements of cards formally grouped or cascading over the surface.

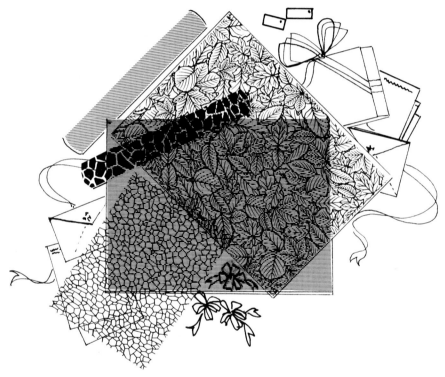

Leather Goods

Leather has always had a certain quality about it, the very smell and appearance of a group of belts, wallets, and handbags gives you an idea of how best to show it. The stress should be made on the quality and the fact that it is natural. Of course a lot depends on the type of goods you are showing. Smart or sophisticated bags and purses in patent or calf will need a different treatment to tan hide luggage or shoulder bags in rough suede. Your display can draw on one of the following techniques.

Clean cut groups or panel displays In Britain I know of no better examples than the displays by the John Lewis leather department. As a general rule leather goods should be grouped very simply. This is best achieved by selecting from ranges of one or two colours. When selecting as with any other gift items, your work will be made that much easier by selecting different heights and sizes, items that will stand and those that will lay flat to form a base perhaps. A sample group might contain a desk blotter, paper knife, letter rack, wallets, credit card case, magazine holder, note pad, memo board, waste bin, spirit flask, pens, and brief case.

Displays of leather goods heightened with other merchandise Gucci, Fortnum & Mason, and Ferragamo have done this type of display brilliantly. If dealing with panel displays, belts and umbrellas are very useful for defining the shape of groups. If possible, silk or woollen scarves can be used in conjunction with bags and gloves. These add colour, texture, and pattern and lend a richness that complements the leather surfaces.

Mood displays In these, an atmosphere is built up around the merchandise. Hermes, Liberty, Harrods, and many other stores feature such displays. Sometimes dramatic displays of leather goods can be arranged using actual hides or skins as background props, this stresses the origins of the merchandise and adds interest. Spotlighting can also bring up the depth of colours we find in leather goods. One of the most exciting and effective displays I have seen was dependent on such an effect. It was quite some time ago and I came across it in Paris. The whole window floor was covered in dry crisp autumn leaves, their golden, reddish colours made a wonderful backing for the bags and luggage in brown leather and deep green suede. A few branches and boughs completed this display. You might say to yourself, very dull and ordinary, but the shafts of light picking out the merchandise and the overall mood and richness still stay in my memory — no mean achievement, after many years of looking at display after display.

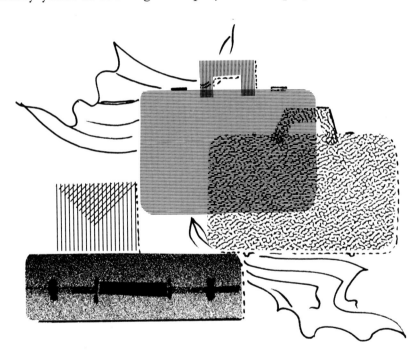

Gifts

I include in the blanket coverage of giftware any groups of small items usually of various shapes and sizes. We could find in a department store's mixed gift displays anything from stationery to a scarf. Probably a Christmas gift display would contain small items of furniture like a magazine rack, tie and trouser press, stools or table lamps. There would almost certainly be a selection of books, videos, records, tapes, cards, calendars, ornaments, jewellery, china, pens, and stationery. The list could go on and the variety would grow depending on the size of the store. Quite small gift shops have the same problem: a large range of mainly uncoordinated merchandise.

We must tackle this situation from the ground up, so to speak. Supports are essential to lift the smaller items and to give some semblance of design to our display. Shelving of any sort is always useful — this can be high tech. or basic depending on the type of shop or situation. Old pine dressers and chests make marvellous stock carriers and lend charm and appeal to the whole effect. If you have a suitable ceiling, shelves can be suspended quite easily. This makes for a very clean uncluttered display leaving the merchandise as the main attraction. Tables and any form of modular system are another solution to the height problem.

You can solve the actual dressing difficulties in two ways. Arrange co-ordinated items in groups, or everything mixed up but grouped to colour. A record sleeve in shades of red could be with a rose coloured lamp, a red glass bottle, fake ruby earrings, a wine coloured ceramic ash-tray, a scarlet box of stationery, a magenta and pink scarf. Work your way through the display and you will be surprised how exciting the different colour groups look. Essential to the success of a mixed gift window or interior is the grasp of playing shape against shape. Contrast textures and patterns and above all get a certain handwriting or sense of order into your grouping and handling.

Work to themes either seasonal or special occasions — this always give more point and impact. Remember not to clutter up your displays with masses of fussy extras — props, showcards, window stickers, and the like only confuse the eye.

Models or figures can be introduced quite easily and give a focus to many gift displays. A bride or child figure can often be incorporated as a focal feature. Fantasy or seasonal figures such as angels, scarecrows, witches, the three wise men, and Father Christmas, have all been used constantly in display work. We can still give them a new twist, a different angle, and feature them in gift displays.

Above: an example showing two linking groups of china and glass displays. Each group is balanced in its own right yet there is an overall balance when the two are combined.

China and Glass

A wealth of patterns and shapes make both glass and china displays interesting to arrange and light. I mention light as this is especially important to consider when we are working with glass.

Let's begin with the usual china sets and services such as the full dinner service or tea or coffee set. Here we are faced with several problems but lots of bonuses. The shapes are very varied and we have the ability to place one item or another if space is short. Six plates laid in a row can be condensed into one stack, and if needed eighteen plates graded in their sizes can stack on the same spot. We have large platters or serving dishes, bowls and flat dishes, cups and saucers and tureens all designed to look good together both in shape and design. The fully laid table is ideal to show off a superb Minton or Royal Doulton dinner service; and a small table laid for tea, or an elegant or modern tray set for coffee are hard to beat. These are not always possible, however, and often we are required to show a range of designs plus gift items such as boxes, vases, or mugs.

Grouping once again is the key to sorting things out as with cosmetics and gifts we are really playing with shapes and sizes. The vertical against the circular, the tall next to the short bowl. The curve of a handle or spout will help the rhythm flow through your arrangements. Study the manufacturers' catalogues and hand outs — it is all there arranged by experts. See how many times our old ally the triangular grouping crops up, enhanced by backgrounds, flowers, or accessories.

Do not let your groupings get too busy. One can be quite regimented, using rows, stacks, and tight groups. If all of these start to merge or get over fussy, the shape and line of the arrangement blur and we lose that essential crisp identity which is an asset to most china displays. There will be exceptions with rose covered plates cascading from wicker baskets, or fun designs that need a pop or young theme. By and large though,

Above: a multi level asymmetric grouping of Royal Worcester cookware, by John Lewis. This style is unbeatable for showing a wide range of stock whilst conveying an uncluttered image. Wine racks and bottles are brought in to add interest.

clearly defined groups, perhaps making up one larger unit, look good.

We can make much of the design features on the china itself by co-ordinating our schemes, backdrops, and staging to harmonize or contrast with the china's colour and design. I like to study the designs that will be on show and lct their patterns and colouring lead my imagination to find a suitable setting. Modern china can be dramatized or heightened enormously by its setting and lighting. We can incorporate vibrant colours and printed cloths to make the most of line, shape and pattern. Examples of this can be found in the Design Centre and specialist china shops like Thomas Goode which feature china in exciting ways and are well worth visiting.

I have talked mainly about china, and thinking in terms of fine bone china or earthenware. There are of course just as many occasions when pottery with a strong earthy or rustic appeal has to be shown. Then I advise that we follow the above guidelines but stress the differing nature of the product by clever use of textures and moods. Props such as wooden crates or plants are ideal. Any natural items such as dried flowers, logs, branches, straw will enhance the pottery and make the display that much more inviting and arresting to the shopper.

Colour, transparency, sparkle, and reflection are all assets when it comes to displaying and lighting glassware displays.

If our chosen products are coloured then it pays to group by colour or by range of the chosen shade, such as ultramarine, pale blue, aqua, turquoise, and violet. This always works and can stop any display of mixed colours looking like a rainbow.

More often than not we have to display clear glass and then we can end up with a sparkling but bleak and anaemic display. A lot depends on background colour and texture. I like to use cool colours such as blues and greys — the deeper the better — to show up the shape and sparkle of simple,

Above: a lightly sophisticated and elegant
display by Liberty of china and glassware.
Merchandise is concentrated in four
areas. The simple triangular panel and
table contribute pattern and focus.

plain, or elaborate cut glass. Of course any colours can be used, but I personally avoid beiges, browns, and warmish tones or shades. Glass to me has a shiny coldness and it looks well against materials like marble, steel, mirror, velvet, or suede. My advice to anyone showing glassware is to experiment with backgrounds and lighting, take a few snaps and compare results. You will be surprised how the same item can be transformed by background and a different light source.

If you study store or shop displays featuring glass, you will often find that whole displays or units are lit from below. Glass really benefits from this technique and collections of rare and valuable glasses are often shown this way in museums or stately homes.

Fabrics and flowers, fresh or artificial can all be used in conjunction with glass displays, depending on design and colour. With modern glass, sheer blinds or dramatic cloths can stress the design qualities. If the glassware is traditional or delicate, then romantic, even fussy settings may be appropriate. The look and feel of the merchandise you have to show will give you vital clues to its presentation.

There can be no hard and fast rules for such a vast field of products. Colour, shape, and the very transparency of the pieces will give you sensational effects that you cannot achieve with any other material. But remember always to clean and polish your stock thoroughly. The resulting gleam and sparkle more than reward your efforts.

Problem Merchandise

The theme running through this book is that no matter what we have to sell or show, or where we are forced to display it, there is always an answer. I would be guilty of over simplifying if I suggested that every merchandise is desirable or a joy to handle. Let us just take a few problem items that will illustrate my point.

Beds and bedding Whilst admitting that beds and mattresses have constantly been improving their visual image, the fact remains that we look at most bedroom displays because we are attracted by the quilt or duvet designs covering the beds. Beds themselves are all on the same level apart from bunk beds. Bedding departments stretch into the distance with a sea of mattresses, all low level. How can we bring interest and a variety of heights into a display or showroom showing only bedding?

Above: this John Lewis bedding display carries a good range of towels and linens. The partitions break up the space. Room setting section shows how a design can look complete with accessories.

We can of course raise beds at angles for interest, but by and large the public likes to see their place of rest in the position in which they will sleep on it. This is particularly so in showrooms where most customers will try the beds. Our only alternative, then, is to glamourise and enhance the beds, we can do this by placing interesting objects or furniture by them. Groups of plants, flowers, cupboards, wardrobes, pictures, mirrors, screens, and such like can all be used to give height or interest.

Raised plinths, carpeted or coloured, can lift the bed physically and aesthetically. We can rig up fake backdrops or canopies that break up monotonous areas. Try to avoid beds in room settings unless they have bedspreads or bed linens on them, then of course they are part of the scheme of decoration. I have seen several interesting bedding display ideas where lightweight boards cut to full bed size are fitted up with sheets and duvets pinned to them. These are hung in repetition or in a group. Pillows and other co-ordinates are displayed in a similar fashion.

Lamps and lighting fittings Hanging lamps or chandeliers in quantity presents many difficulties. We are faced with a mass of items, many of which are hanging at the same height. Lighting shops and departments can, if space allows, create a walk through cavern effect. This can be achieved by grouping the hanging lamps or fittings in staggered column-type arrangements. These can sweep low almost to floor level or meet up and mingle with table lamps or free standing fittings. Using space in this way creates a much more interesting vista through the showroom or shop area. The actual ceiling area gains from the grouping and the overall effect gives definition and a feeling of space. When we are dealing with wall fixtures, this is a much more straightforward procedure.

Displays featuring lamps and lighting fixtures can be handled in much the same way as the instructions above advise. We can choose our stock to display from a variety of ranges — crystal, brass, wood, or ceramics. This, therefore, makes the task much easier as we have a hook on which to hang a theme or colour scheme. Oriental silk shades on pottery or lacquer bases would look well against screens of co-ordinating or matching silks. There are many colour schemes and props that can bring about these mood changes in your displays. Try crystal, glass, and mirrors, flowered chintzes with cottage style lamps. Don't be afraid to be bold with colour, scarlet P.V.C. panels with chromium or black modern fittings will really come to life when the lamps are alight.

Table lamps really do look their best on tables; we can group them, large and small, and raise some on small bases though these latter should be as unobtrusive as possible and are used just to add height. Remember that in a lighting display we can achieve a really dramatic effect not only from the lighting fittings or lamps we are selling but the surfaces that support or are behind them. Metallic, or mirrored surfaces will sparkle and add life — velvets or textures will add colour and

Left: simple wall treatment for lighting track and fittings in the Concord London Showroom. White mannequin creates a focal point and shadows.

depth.

Rugs and Carpets   Here is an area of display work that few relish. Occasionally we are delighted to find a selection of Persian or modern rugs, where the merchandise can be suspended on poles or mounted on panels. Certain more flexible rugs and small carpets can be draped quite easily from the corner. These may be sculpted into interesting shapes or tumbled across chairs, stools, and boxes. Props should be kept simple and strong. On such occasions we can create a theatrical-type setting around our merchandise. An Eastern bazaar would suit a mass of jewel-coloured imported carpets and rugs. Furniture and models in the thirties style would back up designer rugs with an art deco feel.

Generally, however, whilst attractive in themselves, carpets are heavy and awkward to display. We are constricted in some ways by the very nature of the carpet itself, always looking at its best when adorning a room or hotel restaurant. However, we cannot in the display situation show more than one example in this way. We must rely on rolls or columns of carpet grouped in a variety of ways. Samples can be shown in imaginative ways — a mosaic-like wall could feature many designs. Alternatively, we could suspend mounted pattern samples on boards which could be viewed all round, thus enabling more colourings to be shown.

The main point to remember, when displaying huge rolls or pieces of carpet, is to keep it from looking too massive and heavy.

Household electrical equipment   Small items such as vacuum cleaners, food processors, toasters, and shavers all lend themselves to grouping. They relate with many other displays and can often be used as accessories in room settings or gift windows. However, the larger pieces of household elec-

Left: a Concord exhibition stand in white. The glossy white columns make a reception area and create a background. Light fittings are massed onto the tubular framework. The only decoration consists of over a thousand real hyacinths—their fragrance in an exhibition situation made a great talking point.

trical equipment often present us with the problem of variety. Freezers, fridges, and microwave ovens are designed in general to be unobtrusive and fit into a kitchen scheme. Usually with fridge and freezer displays or showrooms a mass of white blocks blinds us, and it is hard to achieve interest or visual impact in this bleak clinical setting. Stereo systems, videos, and televisions also present a similar problem due to lack of variety.

To break this uniformity we can vary our levels by using plinths, platforms, or tables, perhaps based on a modular system. These can be unobtrusive or be coloured to add interest and impact to our scheme. Island sites can face four ways and items can be placed back to back or set against dividers and screens.

Information and any related point of sale material can be suspended and integrated into the groups. Tickets and graphics should be simple and direct. Make sure they are fixed securely and not left to be picked up or knocked down.

Panels and screens can be used; these can be as flimsy or as strong as you need. Suspended banners of lightweight gauze can fill an area with colour or pattern, or carry a logo. Grids or ceiling fixtures are useful in such areas.

All the above techniques can be used in electrical goods displays, care being taken in getting colour, variety, and visual interest into each grouping.

Having been in many display situations, especially on a freelance basis I can assure the reader that in the end, you should view each new merchandise, each new brief from a client in a fairly detached but practical way. Don't be swept away by the prestige or glamour of the goods, likewise look at problem merchandise in an optimistic way. If it is pan scourers and plastic buckets, see them in terms of colour and shape, if it is industrial work wear, try to link it with its function.

Left: exotic grasses and a dramatic seated figure in a display of Eastern carpets and rugs at Browns of Chester. Note the rope and poles over which the large carpet is thrown. The rope motif appears again in the model's hands.

Food and Drink

My main aim here is to give advice to my reader on food shown in special displays, not from the chef's angle, but from the display person's. Entertaining and table or buffet presentation are featured regularly in all the major women's magazines, and books on the subject are in abundance. I advise anyone interested to collect and research this whole field. Magazines such as *Gourmet, À La Carte* and *House and Garden* are an inspiration in themselves. Such topics as colour, garnishes, lighting, and accessories are there on the pages for us to adapt at will. The styling and standard of photography in most cookbooks can also teach us so much about various types of setting, background, and mood for different foods.

I want to concentrate on the types of display we might find in specialist shops or department stores. I believe that in some situations, with food as with fresh flowers, there is no substitute for the real thing. There are always risks if you are using real rather than artificial food, so only when selling from the display, as in the case of cheeses, bread, or confectionery is this advisable. Food that is not packaged or sealed in tins or containers is a very special area of display work. The problems that we encounter when food is put on show are many and vary in degree from discolouration to melting completely under the heat of display lighting. Anyone who has ever prepared a meal or snacks for a party will have some idea of the importance of freshness and cleanliness.

There are imitation foodstuffs available now that are amazing in their lifelike quality. Restaurants can use these profitably with hamburgers, knickerbocker glories, or salads designed and made to look like their product.

We can always sell by mood, setting, or graphics. A display of freshly ground coffee need feature but a handful of beans. Perhaps it might contain giant coffee sacks, good graphics and ticketing, and a prop if needed. The message of fresh coffee comes across. Health foods can be promoted quite successfully using packets or containers, photographs, fresh plants, or dried herbs can add decoration.

Here then is a brief list of some foodstuff displays with suggestions as to props or materials used. This is intended as a guide only and your imagination can take all of these suggestions much further. In some cases, such as with fish, we must have refrigerated slabs, and the correct conditions to keep everything perfect.

Bread and rolls Baskets, rush matting, evergreen foliage, handcarts, pine furniture, hessian, baking trays, gingham, old wagon wheels, brass or copper.

Chocolates — confectionery Giant glass jars or containers, be-ribboned boxes, trays, acrylic dishes or tables, giftwraps, mirrors.

Health foods Fresh foliage, wheat, dried grasses or leaves, twigs, baskets, rustic shelving or logs, slices cut from trees, suitable fabrics in fresh colours and patterns, platters made from natural materials, books.

Wines and spirits Wooden panels, casks, wooden cases, wine racks, fake grapes and fruits, slate, stone, raw timber, evergreens, shelving, mirror tiles, glasses, decanters, lanterns, books, suede, racks, antique furniture.

Dairy produce Fresh straw, wooden shelves and trays, basketry, churns, cheese boards or slabs, marble, old farmyard implements, suitable fabrics with a country feel, wooden planking, racks and hooks, dried herbs and grasses.

Fish and shellfish Shells, tiles, ceramic dishes and platters, figures, sculptures such as mermaids or Neptune, plastic materials, P.V.C., translucent pearlized plastic, metallic foils, ice, nets, cork floats, lobster pots, various baskets, coral, pebbles.

Overleaf: a hard selling massed window of confectionery from Thorntons. Attractive boxes with ribbons and flowers are set on satin drapes against a trellis screen. A turntable showing the contents gives movement.

These displays are mock-ups, created in Thorntons' display studio, then copied throughout their many shops.

Ice creams, summer drinks Patio tables and umbrellas, murals or photos of sea and sun, jugs, artificial ice creams, fans, sunglasses, magazines, holiday brochures, fake fruits, sunhats, towels, deck chairs, trays.

There is little the display person can do with frozen foods stored in special cases. Many of the latest types of containers are so designed that they can accommodate a variety of goods all easily viewable for self selection. These are just filled up as items sell and need no special display skill. Wall mounted units with glass doors do the same job and do, at least, make the area more interesting from the shopper's viewpoint. Signs and graphics should be kept clear, clean, and simple in these situations. Colours should stand out and tie in with the overall scheme of the area. Sometimes wall panels of dummy packs or free standing displays featuring fridges and freezers are incorporated if space allows. These can be made to look attractive and colourful with added props or fake foods giving colour and a focal point in what can be a rather bleak and clinical setting.

Food display is a specialist field and the resulting sales from good, imaginative presentation are well worth the effort. It is an area where we must be scrupulously clean and hygenic for both aesthetic and health reasons. Remember our main objective with all food and drink display is to whet the appetite visually.

Flowers and Foliage

I would strongly advise any would-be display practitioner to study the art of flower and foliage arrangement. Some time ago, I was asked to lecture to a group of flower arrangement teachers on the use of backgrounds, colour, and fabrics. I was not prepared for the searching questions, the sheer artistry and skill that I encountered. So many professionals in our field view the world of flower arrangement with tongue-in-cheek, something to be carried out in churches and country shows, at best one step removed from floristry and the hotel lounge.

Nothing could be further from the truth. I spent many years visiting and lecturing to flower clubs all over the country. I learnt more from classes, demonstrations, conferences, and national shows than I ever did from any display person. Our guidelines such as balance, line, use of colour, suitability, and scale of setting all run parallel to the world of the flower arranger. Some aspects of the craft appeared rather forced and constricting but generally I found flower arrangement was wonderfully flexible and led people into many related areas.

We, in display, are forced by the nature of our work to use mostly artificial material as this will last. On occasions there comes the chance to use fresh flowers, plants, or a mixture of both 'pot en fleur'. If this is possible, I would advise its use. Nothing gives the same effect as a fresh bloom or living plants. Recently I saw a window covered in grey felt showing modern heavy silver jewellery and cutlery. Its only foil was three pots of cinneraria in deep blue, cerise, and violet — the effect was stunning.

As I have stated, if one wants to improve one's skill or perception and knowledge of flowers as decoration, there are books and clubs to read or join. Apart from the enjoyment of stretching one's own knowledge, a deeper love and understanding of all growing things in the garden or countryside is very rewarding.

Christmas

Christmas is the major display event in our year and accounts for a large portion of trading profits with many shops and stores. It is the time for the big effect. We can pull out all the stops, go right over the top on occasions. Our work can be especially rewarding when geared towards children. Animated displays, grottos, and tableaux are gazed at in wonder by the children and grown-ups for the two months preceding the holiday. Many stores are well into their Christmas planning in early summer and some companies start thinking the full year ahead. There are certain shops in America which sell nothing but Christmas items the whole year round.

While it is considered very smart to create a Christmas scheme that bears no relationship to the festival at all, even the most up market companies usually come back down to earth with a traditional scheme every so often. I list here some of the usual symbols and themes that we encounter yearly in our high streets and shopping precincts.

Trees of all types, pine, spruce, fir, artificial, metallic, coloured.
Angels, sculpted, fibre glass, fabric, paper, wooden.
The Three Kings, dressed figures, painted, fake stained glass.
Stars, tinsel, illuminated, plastic, metallic, jewelled.
Holly, real, satin, plastic, paper, painted.
Fir cones, giant real, plastic.

As Christmas displays can take in practically all types of merchandise, refer to the sections describing techniques for your own merchandising problems. There are several well worn but nonetheless workable ideas that I can suggest. Tree shapes cut from planking shelves filling in the area to hold gifts. Large tree, or bauble shapes cut from foam core board and painted or covered, use these as panels. Sacks and stockings can be fun especially cut giant size, but they are not very useful when it comes to arranging merchandise.

Right: this Turnbull and Asser display continues the Jermyn Street tradition of crisply ruched shirtings framing a wealth of men's items suggested as gifts. A humourous note comes in the form of the scarf bedecked reindeer head.

Sales

The magic of words like *bargain, reduced, clearance, sale*, still have amazing effects on the spending public. Whereas not so long ago the January Sales or end of season fashion clearance was a regular feature in most shops and stores — a good way to clear out of date or damaged stock — now the Sales are a major part of many stores' marketing strategy with millions of pounds or dollars being spent at the bigger department stores.

The media play a great part in the success of Sales. For weeks before Christmas each year we find hints of preparations. News coverage features people queueing through many nights and days, for themselves or fund raising for a charity. Mothers and children are fed with bowls of soup, or something stronger by some of the more up market companies. All this builds up an excitement that floods through the high streets and cities the moment Christmas is over. It is easy to see why sales are so popular, especially the winter ones. Most people love a bargain and January can be a pretty bleak month both for trading and the weather. What better fill-in, then, than to slap up posters and give the public a good excuse to spend savings or gift money?

The problems with most Sale displays are the usual ones of not enough space, too little time to spend, and the ability to keep the pot boiling, as it were, by replacing things removed from the display. If the bargains are good, the window can literally be stripped bare in the first day — in some cases in the first ten minutes. With everybody working like mad selling, and crowds of shoppers pushing and jostling, the window can often be cleared and left empty for hours. This is good for sales, but bad from the display angle. Try at all costs to have replacements ready for the sold items. This can be organized before the shop opens.

The message that a Sale is on must be spelt out loud and clear. The bargain hunters are not the types who stroll along drinking in the visual and subtle delights usually offered by our work. Signs large and loud are what they are on the lookout for. I have known a shop that placed drastically reduced merchandise in the window but omitted the magic word *Sale* only to find little response to its efforts. The same merchandise sold instantly after a Sale banner was slapped onto the glass.

Preparation, as with any other form of display work, is vital where Sale displays are concerned. If at all possible, find out exactly what is going to be featured, especially the star bargains or special offers. Remember that price is a prime factor in any Sale display so ticketing is very important — clearly written or printed tickets with reductions clearly shown are always an asset. Giant showcards or posters with a blanket coverage caption written on them, such as 25% off everything, work well and attract attention.

Avoid complicated fixtures, stands, or fittings — speed in removing and replacing is essential, and all merchandise should be shown as simply as possible. Racks, shelves, hangers, rails, and hooks can all be featured. Try not to use suspension, pinning, draping, or any time consuming methods of handling.

Remember, when dealing with small items or large groups of boring individual objects, to use the mass effect to its full. Stacks of tins or mugs are far more eye catching than half a dozen on a shelf. Baskets filled to overflowing with knitting yarns or Christmas decorations look much more exciting than a few items laid on the window base. Study techniques used in the outdoor markets. Upturned boxes or simple frameworks pinned or lashed together can carry all sorts of stock. Fabrics or towels can be thrown over bars, fixed or suspended.

If possible keep the Sale windows interesting and full, it is all too easy to let things slide after the initial rush. It is hard to make an impact with a half full window of tired left over merchandise but our job is to do just that, condense, re-group, and generally keep an eye on the stock situation.

To sum up, Sales are not the most rewarding time for our efforts, but they are good for business and that is what our job is all about. Remember, too, that Sales are the trade's way of clearing the decks, a sort of spring cleaning, making way for new stock, new ideas, and exciting displays.

Garden Centres

This book has mainly concerned itself with shops, stores, and showrooms — in fact all covered locations or sites. There are those whose great concern is not floor coverings, lighting, and such like but the elements themselves. In the British climate especially, open sites are vulnerable to extremes of weather. This fact has been made abundantly clear to me recently. I have lectured to many regional groups brought together by The Agricultural Training Board. Their main concern was garden centre displays — an area until now sadly neglected by owners and managers of many garden centres. This particular problem of coping with exterior display areas has triggered off a whole new aspect of my job as a consultant and teacher.

Naturally, displays in the open are not going to imitate those inside, yet colour, backgrounds, grouping, and ticketing must all still be considered. The main differences occur when we start to choose the materials we use for stands, for gaining height, or covering substances.

There are many modern materials that we can use both inside and outside. P.V.C. can be purchased in a range of colours from display suppliers. A range of waterproof fabrics is available in nylon and other manmade fibres. Canvas and other materials used in connection with boats are worth looking at. Acrylic sheeting can be brought into play and will take logos or lettering. Above all once you have decided on a style — a colour or scheme — take it all the way. It may take months even years to achieve that look, that image you seek, but you are on the right path.

Flexibility's our greatest asset if working with plants or natural products such as wood and stone: paving slabs, fencing, bamboo canes, foliage and colour can be brought together in a thousand ways that please the eye. A visit to The Chelsea Flower Show will prove this point or a look at any book on great gardens landscaped by experts.

All too often though, we are faced by messy areas in

Left and on following pages: a garden centre bang in the heart of Chelsea drawing on display techniques. Plant groupings and structures are brought together to add variety and interesting vistas. Paved areas make a perfect foil for tubs and furniture. Trellis is used in a structural and decorative fashion. Graphics and signs play an important part in the overall effect.

garden centres where one section merges into another. Sometimes a beautiful display of urns, pedestals, statues, and pots has been decimated after selling some items, leaving a sad, forgotten aspect. In huge garden centres, where expert staff look after such areas as floristry, plants, catering, and finance, it is surprising that there is more often than not no one responsible for the appearance of the place. It is not enough to talk to experts and employ designers to create logos, and colour schemes. These may give you an initial boost and a good image, but unless a continuous day to day servicing is organised and carried out, things degenerate rapidly.

There are trouble-free units, floorings, and covering materials which can make the whole business look and work that much better. We only have to take stock of the products a garden centre sells to realise the benefits of plastics, resins, wipe clean surfaces, and glass substitutes.

If we are careful and plan our display areas so that they will easily adapt to our seasonal requirements, we have won part of the battle. As an example, I visited a garden centre where raised stone platforms had been firmly cemented into place in several areas. In the summer these were covered with bedding plants, in the winter they were just piled with bags of peat and a few odd potted shrubs. Personally I would have preferred twenty or so concrete screen blocks, and eight lengths of seasoned planking, the rougher the better. With these I could have formed units that take trays of plants, pots, shrubs, in fact most things. Flexibility is a great asset, and components that can be moved around like a child's construction set are great for such purposes. There is, of course, the added bonus that, poles, trellis, screens, slabs, pots, or whatever else you use can be sold afterwards if no longer needed.

Garden centres are a wonderful place to find display props and aids. Apart from the items I have mentioned, take a look at the potential in sheet polythenes, meshes, nets, wire arches,

fencing, polypropolene ropes in bright colours, screens and panels of wood or plastics. I know of many display persons who would be delighted to select props from these.

The garden centre of today is simply a type of department store that is just out of town or deep into the countryside. With the added sophistication of many new departments, we find silk flowers, gourmet foods, gift wraps, cards, wine departments and health foods alongside the bulbs and composts, the shrubs and weedkillers. Suffice it to say then that the presentation has to have a shake up inside and out. Large areas are given over to the promotion of seasonal goods, bulb planting, barbecues, and bird feeders. Christmas is now a busy period in their calendar, and some centres feature it very strongly indeed — it was a quiet time a few years back, but now a market for trees, decorations, and grottos has been created and increased.

The wolves are at the door, however, and there is much competition around. The D.I.Y. chains and other big companies have their eyes and fingers on this lucrative market, this is why it is so essential for garden centres to shout not whisper their unique qualities. In America the whole business is in much better shape, but things here are improving. As someone who loves gardens and flowers, I can think of nothing nicer than to drive into a good garden centre that is attractively laid out. Take a stroll through the various departments and outside areas, perhaps be tempted to purchase a shrub or tree, then take refreshments in a pleasant coffee shop or restaurant area. This is a completely different activity for a family, than shopping in a busy precinct or shopping centre. The way the garden centre looks will play a large part in its appeal and success. Displays can make dull areas interesting and awkward or unsightly sections can be masked by careful screening. Vistas and planned customer flow walkways can lead people through all the sections in a subtle but profitable way.

Signage, a dreadful word but very descriptive I am afraid, is of tremendous importance. Who has not had the experience of visiting a garden centre and finding themselves in a labyrinth of trees and plants? Worse still a barren view with no indication as to where to go to find special items. I will agree it is not easy to achieve height but when you have everything flat or on ground level and the place is busy, problems occur. Giant flowers, signposts, pavilions, or simple notice boards raised, preferably as part of a display or feature, can help. These can be made from interesting and sympathetic materials on posts or poles, even cemented into pots or tubs. Many garden centres do a wonderful job — external notices are sealed against the elements, signs are high and easily read. There are quite a lot, however, whose faded, stained, curling posters and information panels are very much in evidence. It is not an easy task to keep everything in a garden centre looking just right, but it does make a tremendous difference to the look and feel of the site.

5: Materials and Props

Junk as Props

The inventive display person will be able to utilise all manner of objects, junk, disposable packaging, or industrial waste materials to achieve unusual and exciting displays. Then, drawing on a concept such as contrast, use of like with like, or of surprise can lend structure to the choice of props.

Contrast This could mean silk scarves or fabrics arranged on barbed wire or machinery parts; jewellery on a bed of bricks or coal; or glamorous evening wear or lingerie shown against industrial metal sheeting. The idea is not to shock or surprise but to play textures and moods against each other for effect. It works in a similar way to colour theory in that bright flashes of red are set off perfectly by dark forest-green. Silk and precious metals look their best against hessian, jute, or suede. Painters use this technique very often when dealing with still life groupings. Linen cloths against gleaming pewter and luscious fruits against rough stone or flaking plaster — these achieve their effects by contrasts.

Like on like This is the very opposite, but works most effectively if executed well. White merchandise against white backgrounds or fixtures, with raised graphics or captions also in white, can be most eye catching. I have seen this idea maybe a hundred times in my career used in displays and fashion presentations and in nearly every case it looks good. Schemes that are composed of a single colour (monochromatic) or varying tones of that colour fall into this category. Sometimes a bold pattern can be the focus of a display. A striped floor and walls, with plinths or boxes covered in yet another stripe, makes a very powerful statement visually. Spots or zebra patterns work well and they can be created with paint, collage, or simply from patterned papers or fabrics. A viewing of some old Rodgers and Astaire and Busby Berkley films will reinforce my points about the decorative effects of pattern. Floors and

Preceding page: hands are timeless, and these larger than life examples from Propaganza make a useful prop to illustrate the point.

costumes, even people were used to create static and moving patterns.

The surprise element One thinks of gravity defying displays where everything in a room setting is stuck upside down to the ceiling of a window or display area. Whole areas of glass blacked out or masked with a small aperture engaging the public's curiosity to step closer and peer in. Live people in every guise have been used as statues, window dummies, or robots to stop the passer-by. One major retailer in this country has blocked out the complete window areas with posters to feature their summer Sale.

We can if we do our homework correctly look back and be inspired by some of the truly innovative artists and creative souls who have led the way. The early work of Cecil Beaton, Christian Berards's brilliant stage sets and drawings, and the works of Louise Nevelson. Dali's surrealistic fantasies, are pure display, as are clearly defined colours and spaces in a Mondrian painting. Braque, Schwitters, Bridget Riley, Hockney, and hundreds more use pattern, surfaces, colour, and materials in their own original way stamped with their own style.

Here then as a summary to this basic idea of using unexpected or novel materials is a personal list of just a few avenues to explore.

Factory and industrial waste

Metal shavings
Plastic sheeting or offcuts
Yarns and spools
Building materials
Packaging materials
Wood wool packaging
Sheet plastics and

Tubes and piping
Bubble wrap
Shredded cellophane or plastic
Rusting metal sheeting
Boxes, all shapes and sizes

polythene
Springs
Card and paper waste

Angle iron
Packing crates
Corrugated cardboard

Natural materials

Rocks
Trees, twigs, or branches
Old wooden beams
Wood shavings
Rushes and grasses
Pebbles
Corn
Raw timber from sawmill

Sand
Bullrushes
Driftwood
Dried leaves
Sawdust
Peat
Bamboo

Found or man-made items

Old machinery or car parts
Junk furniture
Rope and netting of any type
Sheeting materials
Glass substitutes

Bed springs
Tea chests
Chicken wire
Old dressmaker's dummies
Old ladders and steps
Barbed wire

Left: an elaborate table centre for a huge banquet designed by the author. Twenty-foot-long boards were laden with all manner of objects, toys, fruits, fake foods, and such like. The whole arrangement was sprayed white, then, vivid aniline varnishes were applied in reds, violets, and magentas. Jewels and sequins were the final embellishment.

Above: a giant totem pole with a decorative border, all made from paper, at the Paperpoint exhibition.

Ready-made Materials

In the section devoted to making props from junk or using industrial waste I am obviously aiming at display people who are or want to be creative — making, painting, and shaping objects or backgrounds to use in their displays. A much larger proportion of my readers, I am sure, does not have the time or inclination for such goings on.

When we need schemes ready-made and delivered we can turn to the specialist manufacturers who make props and aids for the display profession. The Germans have the edge on most people when it comes to supplying a whole package to make a seasonal display.

The actual materials we use in display are quite basic and most of them are borrowed from other specialist fields. Once again the display house will usually stock felt, hessian, muslin, P.V.C., and a range of covering fabrics or effects. Fake velours, brushed suedes, furs and weaves are available. Papers come in many guises from moire silk to Japanese grass effects. Reflecting foils and photographic or screen printed panoramas are always on show in many designs suitable for a variety of merchandise.

Above: polystyrene formers like these by Graham Sweet intended for fabric draping are quick to dress and light to carry. Especially useful where long runs of fabrics are to be treated like curtains.

Covering and Using Panels

Panels, whether framed, unframed, wall mounted, suspended, laid flat, or fixed at angles, are an economical and attractive way to show merchandise. They can carry the actual goods or information plus logos, captions, and any special promotion information. As an alternative they can, in their own right, make an important contribution to a display. They can be brought into play as backgrounds floors, ceilings, screens, or dividers, at the same time tying in or contrasting with the overall scheme. Use textures, patterns, and colours either boldly or in a discreet and subtle fashion depending upon what you are showing.

We are inclined to think of panels as being rectangular or square. This is true in many cases but in the display man's hands he can make them practically any shape he chooses. Triangles, circles, ovals, free shapes — the possibilities are practically endless. These more unusual shapes can be harder to cover or decorate and care must be taken with the finish. First, make sure the fabric, or covering material is straight and cut to size. Then staple or fix with pins or adhesive at North, South, East and West points tensioning the covering as you go. Work around the panel now fixing a few inches at a time on each edge, working all the time towards the corners. Make sure to keep stretching. Cut surplus, and fold or mitre corners. Finally, press or brush the surface as necessary.

Above: fantasy face by the author. This was a prototype to be printed onto white glazed cotton blinds for a series of displays.

Above: these screens add pattern and excitement to displays of business suits. Screen Plan by Formwood.

Above and left: three felt covered panels, used to demonstrate to students, inexpensive and quick methods of applying pattern. Black paint was dribbled onto the white felt in rhythmical sweeping movements. A cheap sponge roller was charged with black emulsion, then rolled across the white felt surface. Leaf shaped stencils were cut from thick paper, a paint filled sponged was then dabbed onto the surface. All three panels were completed within thirty minutes.

Above: arrangement of Kitchen Devil knife using background in a subtle way. The solo knife is accessorised with a cut loaf, butter, and wooden board—the mood strengthened by showing the group on a bed of grain.

Right: covered or in plain card, sets of tubes and platforms like these made by Woking Paper Tubes are invaluable when arranging groups of small items. Easily painted or surface decorated this type of display aid makes co-ordination very easy.

Covering and Using Boxes and Drums

Cubes, boxes of various dimensions, drums, and cylinders are always very useful display aids. They can give us a variety of heights and levels which helps enormously with the arrangement of small items. The covering materials can be as colourful and varied as you choose and the process of covering is relatively simple. It is a good idea to have sets of blocks or drums made which fit into each other like a set of children's stacking blocks. This allows both a selection of varying heights and easy storage. Some companies will either cover in the fabrics of your choice or sell the drums and blocks uncovered.

Covering drums   Paper, felt, or fabric can be wrapped around and glued or stapled at the back. Most fabrics can do this job quite well, but the more stretch the better, as this allows good tension making for a tighter fit. Ends can be folded in and stuck or stapled. Discs of hardboard or wood can be covered to form tops. Larger tops can be covered giving the effect, when assembled, of tables.

Blocks and cubes   These are rather more difficult to cover and are best treated in the manner one would wrap a parcel. Remember that in many cases the tops and bottoms will not show. A sleeve of paper or fabric is enough to achieve an effect. Your blocks and drums can be painted, textured, stained, or dyed in any number of ways but be sure that you choose coverings to fit in and co-ordinate with your scheme. They are not to be a feature in themselves, but simply play their part in showing off the merchandise.

Above: a circle of board and a tube or box to support it transforms into this charming table. The top is fabric covered to match the walls. The skirt is gathered net with a border pattern gathered over a darker plain fabric. This idea is from The Curtain Net Advisory Bureau.

Tables

Basic and everyday as it may appear to us the simple table —
a top with four legs or a central column — is and always has
been a display classic. Trestles or folding tables that stack
away are ideal. These can be given the full treatment or simply
be masked with cloth thrown over them. From such basic
beginnings we can create all manner of stalls or banquets.
Alternatively we can add rods of poles to the corners and fix
cross members, which once again transforms the whole effect
when tented, or canopied with ribbons.

Circular tables in various heights are a useful way to gain
a set of levels in a showroom or display. Cloths can fall to the
ground, and can be made from just a circle of felt with little
or no stitching; more tailored covers can be fashioned from
patterned chintzes or plain cottons.

We can also use rough wooden or rustic tables, planks of
raw timber, marble slabs, or sheets of mirror. If possible and
suitable we can lay our merchandise on antique or repro-
duction tables. The stock and its mood or style will dictate the
needs. Modern tables as with any prop or support may be
exciting, colourful, and well designed, they should, however,
never upstage the merchandise that they are showing.

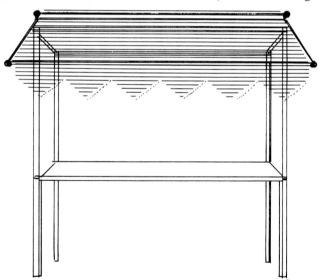

Above: a basic table can be adapted into
a festive stall complete with canopy. Poles
can be fixed to legs with adhesive tapes,
cross pieces tacked on, and fabric
canopy cut and stapled into position.

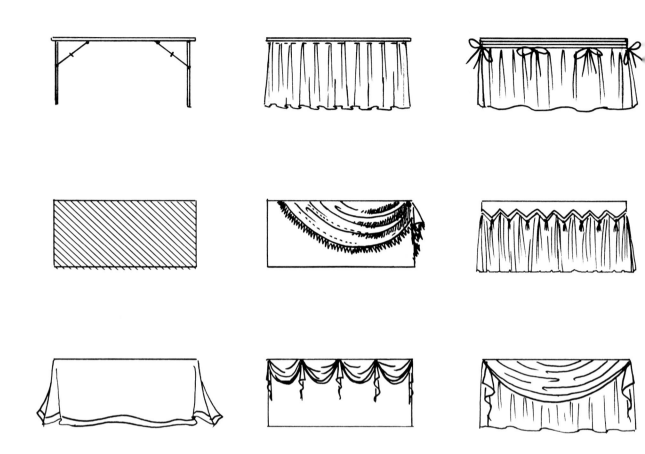

Above: variations on the table theme. A basic pasting table transforms into a number of plain or fancy options by draping or pleating fabrics.

Modular Units — Instant Displays

Such is the wealth of ready made self assembly units available today, that there is no need to advise the reader on how to use them. At exhibitions like SHOPEX we find a great variety of manufacturers exhibiting variations on a theme. Choosing the right one is the problem so look at as wide a range as you can.

Many systems merge into a background by nature of their neutral colour and design features. Others that rely on strong shapes or a fun image, colour, or pattern may look interesting and fresh for eighteen months then date suddenly. Do not be oversold on a unit's versatility, it may well change from a wall into a platform or a spinning roundabout. This won't help you in the slightest if your product or merchandise does not look good with it.

Certain rules will guide you in your choice. If you have masses of information or graphics to show, a system with panels is essential. Textiles would need rods or hanging fixtures and so on. Flexibility is a good thing and I favour personally systems that can break up and come together in different ways.

Certain systems are intended to be mobile: packed flat they can be put in a car or van, opened they look like complex structures and can take all manner of goods. Lightweight materials are used a great deal now and this has made the task of erecting and lifting much easier. One person can cope quite easily with many modern systems, and when the pressure is on for time or staffing, this is a good point to note.

Many schemes are based on a slotted panel with grooves or metal reinforced slots which can take a wide range of fittings. This means that a box shaped area with walls clad in these materials can transform into practically any merchandising area you want. Rails, and rods for fashion, shelves, brackets, and bars can take soft or hard goods as you please. Central pillar or plinth units can be made from the material so a complete shopfitting job can be effected quite simply. The finished appearance is dependent on the colour or texture of the base material. Wood, white melamine, or metallic finishes create different environments that suit many moods or merchandising situations. This type of system has proved very popular, particularly in department stores, as it can change overnight from, say, a sports department to a bookshop or children's clothing area.

The Figure in Display

Models, whether of plaster, resin, or papier mâché, have always played a prominent part in displays in Europe and America. Fashions and trends come and go and still the figures return with ever changing faces and poses. Todays models are a far cry from the static but charming Eton cropped models of the 20s with their bee stung lips and svelte poses.

In the whole field of visual merchandising, the model manufacturers have led the way with their ideas. The use of the figure in a display can add an extra dimension of interest. It humanizes merchandise, and the shopper or viewer at once relates to the product or promotion. A beautifully gowned mannequin can add impact and sex appeal to a display of perfumes or cosmetics. Likewise fantasy figures or comic characters can arrest our attention just by being there.

Not only are models a great aid in many dress fashion schemes, they are also widely used in fabric promotions. Abstracted and natural models can both be used with fabrics but I prefer figures in this branch of display work not to look too realistic. All white or metallic finished models make a wonderful foil for textures and patterns. When using naturalistic models there is a great temptation to show off our expertise and emulate a real dress or garment. When this is done despite the brilliance and skill shown in the handling, we often lose the feel and mood of the fabric itself. We are not selling a finished garment but an idea of how the material could look. The model is there as a prop, an aid to the fabrics on show, and as such it gives the fabric from the roll life and interest. Figures used with fabrics can be as unusual or extremes as the manufacturer or display person can make them. Period tableaux, space age, or ethnic groupings can be created with figures and fabrics alone.

There are so many ways that we can incorporate models into our displays, exhibitions, and showrooms. The attraction value is tremendous and should never be taken for granted.

Left: figures as props. This dramatic and beautifully dressed example is from Adel Rootstein's New York showroom.

One leading multiple in Great Britain fills their Sale windows before the opening day with mannequins covered from head to foot in white sacks, their name printed on the front. These create interest and customers await their removal on Sale day.

Fringe boutiques, and some of the more way out individual shops will often go to extremes for effects. Recently I've seen models hanging upside down from cords, graffiti sprayed figures, male models springing out from trash cans, and female models in men's suits. The public are bemused and the purists will shrug off such oddities, but I think that experiment is a good thing and keeps us on our toes. We are so closely linked with the world of fashion and the trends that come and go that we must join in and in some cases lead the way.

We are almost spoilt for choice when we come to select and purchase model ranges and the various manufacturers tempt us in the most beguiling ways. As a guide I would suggest you base your choice on these four criteria:

Budget How much can I spend and will I get full use from the selection?

Image Are they projecting the right image for the clothes they will be wearing? The right style for the particular shop or store?

Dating Will they date quickly or do I need the look that says NOW?

Renovation Check on repair and renovation. New colours and make-up can create a completely fresh set of figures for you.

For the small shop owner, who cannot compete with the larger stores, choosing figures would be a major decision. Therefore, take time, have a good look around at the ranges available. Weigh up the factors I've described and then choose. Classic need not be dull. The extravagant pose or features may

Left: the designer can slip back in time to the 20s or 30s with display figures like these from Propaganza.

be a knock out in the showroom but think ahead and visualise the same model week after week in a series of different outfits and settings — will this look boring and stale to your customers? On the other hand if your finances can run to it then make a splash with a complete change of model from time to time. (Your discarded set will sell readily if it is looked after.) Some of the most talked about series of displays use specially ordered models, whose make-up and hair styling are an integral part of the overall scheme.

Movement and Animation

There has always been room in the display world for the gimmick, the unusual, the surprise. Animation has been used for many years in one form or another: live models midst static ones, animated puppets, or revolving turntables.

Personally I tread warily when clients or students want to feature movement of one sort or another in their schemes. Having been involved with turntables that just will not turn, rocking motors that do not rock, fountains that leak or spray everything in sight, and walking figures that look deformed and move eratically, I am naturally suspicious. Maintenance is essential and do ensure that an expert company supply and install everything.

I respond, rather, to animation in its more subtle forms. The interplay of moving or coloured lights can create an interesting shimmer of highlights and shadows. Fans concealed behind screens or in the wings, so to speak, of a fabric or fashion window can create interest — the soft fluttering of light fabrics is eye catching and can impart a dramatic or romantic mood. Graphics and words can gain in their effect if they move. A symbol suddenly transforms into a word, then miraculously turns back into a symbol. Projected images that move, brand names that gleam and glow. All these, I feel add another dimension to a static presentation.

There are times, however, when the sudden movement or

Left: figures as props for fabric displays by students. Shields and swords lend an authentic period feel to these figure drapes.

Above: a delightful picture of a New York store display of 1921. The dressmaker's dummy was useful then and indeed has come and gone out of fashion in display work ever since.

the gimmicky idea are needed, when promotions are really helped by the flashing lights, the joky effect, a nodding Santa, or an inflatable clown that laughs and collapses pneumatically, only to rise again for another laugh. However, always be careful that the animation does not cheapen your product, that it looks professional.

New technology has changed the possibilities of animation enormously. The world of computers and electronics, lasers and the field of holography are all waiting to be tapped to their full extent by anyone in the presentation business. It may not suit our particular needs at present, but we should keep our eyes and minds open and receptive to new ideas.

Above: light itself forms the focal feature in this fabric display. Bright yellow neon lettering frames the native hanging. Models themselves echo the theme with suitable wigs and jewellery at Liberty.

Lighting

Inspired lighting can transform the ordinary, even the ugly, into a set piece of great beauty and interest.

Lighting sources for many years were hidden away, then, in the sixties and seventies, as windows opened up and display areas were treated as part of a shop interior, fittings were featured. No longer was the window treated like a stage with proscenium and wings masking our lighting effects. Spotlights and track were, in many cases, the framework or even part of the display itself. By the late seventies this went as far as it could go. Old photographs and magazines reveal displays of hard and soft goods where it seems that it is the spotlights which are being featured. Design has improved now and although there may well be a selection of fittings used in a given area, they can be a feature by their design, and still do a good job. The merchandise, or whatever is being illuminated and promoted, is left as the main focus of attention, the lighting fittings playing a discreet part in the finished picture.

When choosing lighting — be it an installation involving many fittings and areas, or a showcase with a spotlight or two — take expert advice.

Systems and fittings ideally should be an integral part of the whole display area, be it showroom, museum, or exhibition. If it is at all possible to have some say in the type and variety of lighting fixtures to be installed, then remember and take note of what you want from your fittings. Ask yourself what performance you need in terms of heat, distance, and spread of beam. Analyse your needs for certain special types of light fittings — beams that pin point tiny objects, or framing spots that illuminate a picture, a face, or a logo.

Flexibility is always a great asset. We do not install new lighting systems all that often and we will want to ring the changes to add variety and interest to our displays.

There is much competition within the lighting industry on cost effective equipment and fittings, so keep up with new

Right: lighting at the National Theatre is enhanced by the illuminated skyline and the reflections on the water.
Lighting from below a subject can exploit textures and contours. Note how this wall-grazing effect is used on the first floor pillars. The display person can adapt this by using floor spots.

developments. The latest introductions of longer lasting lamps which use far less electricity could well be the deciding factor for your next assignment or purchase. Lighting is not cheap to install or use and manufacturers are aware of this. Many systems and types of fitting are now aimed at the lower budget, high performance needs of our trade.

The sculptural qualities that certain placements of light sources can give to a group of objects are oft neglected weapons in our armoury. A walk along your high street will more often than not mean window after window of flatly lit displays. This can be attributed to a wide use of fluorescent fittings, which, of course, are cheap to run but sadly lacking in any sparkle or interesting effects.

Consider how from a darkened area we can shape and create almost any effect with light. Suddenly, with modern developments, it is possible to wash entire areas with moving patterns or coloured light. Lighting can point up, or play down, it can add colour, movement, pattern, images. If we want a flat grouping given depth and interest it can be achieved. We can add sparkle, reflections, play with timing devices or optical effects. Names, logos, and sales messages can be featured or heightened, precious objects can be bathed in an aura of light. Walls or whole areas can be painted in different shades with light.

Points to remember   Make sure your lighting is working for you night and day. Time switches and a carefully worked out programme are well worth the trouble. Check constantly that as displays are changed so spotlights and fittings are re-positioned for the new arrangements. Don't feature unim-portant items, for example, there is no point in flooding a plain wall with light, or spotlighting an empty floor area. Check that dead lamps are replaced as soon as is possible. Keep track and all fittings clean and polished or dusted. Heat attracts dust and grime. Order a good stock of spare lamps so

Right: this clean cut interior at Heals demonstrates a well lit area. Note the light travelling through the glass shelves and extensive use of downlighters.

that you have a constant supply when the need arises.
Remember you can't always rely on wholesalers or shops
having your particular lamps in stock. Double check on the
suitability of certain lighting for specific items that may be
damaged through heat or light such as soaps or candles which
can melt; pressurised containers which can explode; antiques
and carpets with delicate colours; or veneers that could fade
or lift.

Above: high drama in this Liberty fashion display. A mirror-like floor and angular screens heighten the atmosphere. Models are lit in suitable theatrical manner.

Right: dramatic lighting achieved by a block of fluorescent tubes directly above the gold mask, for the Tutankhamun Exhibition at The British Museum. This method works well on some metals and brilliant objects. Underneath the tubes are low glare cellular louvres. Designer Robin Wade.

Left: the huge mask is dramatized by light. Pencil beams glaze the surfaces ensuring the surrounding areas are darkened, which adds impact to the whole gallery. The Gold of Eldorado Exhibition at the Royal Academy. Designer Alan Irvine.

Above: a fashion window pared down to the bare essentials. Take note of the subtle touches that play second fiddle, the dramatic use of shadow, and the cracked cubes lit from within. Typical Liberty placement of the two models making the most of the space.

6: Display Training and General Information

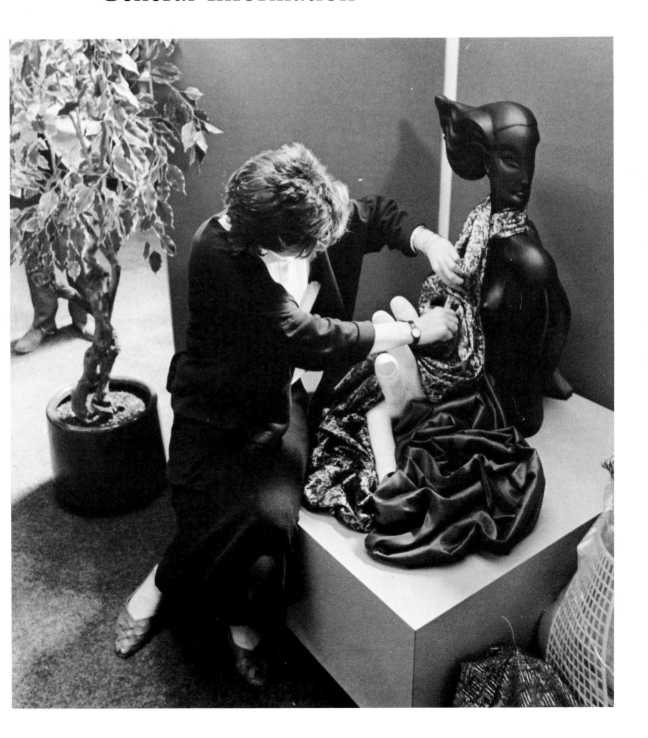

Most people entering display in Britain are recruited from courses in colleges offering certificate and diploma qualifications in display design. These full-time courses cover at least two years' study. The examining bodies associated with such courses are:

Business & Technician Education Council (BTEC)
(England & Wales)
Central House, Upper Woburn Place
London WC1H OHH

Scottish Vocational Education Council (SCOTVEC)
(Scotland only)
38 Queen St
Glasgow G1 3DY

British Display Society (BDS)
Guardian House 92–94 Foxberry Rd
London SE4 2SH

The BDS also offers a Technician Certificate for part time or evening study. Currently there are no advanced courses available in display. Information on the availability of courses can be obtained from the Design Council booklet *Design Courses in Britain* published annually.

Preceding page: a display student tries her hand at fabric sculpture.

Display Course

Within the typical syllabus of a BTEC course of display design, we find quite naturally that the core of the course is based on design and merchandise presentation. Every aspect of these is covered from the basics of theory and lay out, right through merchandise manipulation to marketing strategy.

Graphics play quite a large part in many of the cross module assignments as do all aspects of decoration, colour, pattern, and the study of materials. Many projects stretch the students' artistic gifts, but they are made aware that art is not their main concern. The commercial aspect of the job is always kept to the forefront of the programme and students are encouraged to look closely at the trade itself. Work experience with stores, studios, and styling departments is arranged and at least one three-week period is compulsory in the students' second year. Competitions and projects are set regularly and sometimes sponsored by the trade itself. This creates a real sense of participation and immediacy. A student will be guided through the course by a tutor and assessments are held at regular intervals to monitor progress. Studios and workshops play a large part in the students' work. Full scale realizations are completed of displays and interiors. These are recorded in slide or photograph form and contribute to the all important folio of work that each student builds up over the two-year course. Communication and marketing studies are integrated into many of the assignments to give students an idea of the business world awaiting them.

There are no guarantees for finding employment but every help is given arranging and advising interviews with would-be employers. Open days, seminars, and workshops all keep colleges in close touch with the needs of industry.

Following page: student entries for the British Display Society SHOPEX competition. The theme was based on the European Community.
Menswear is dressed in a casual fashion on three plywood shapes. The panel carries a photo blow-up in black and white. Merchandise featured the red, white, and green of the Italian flag. Italian bikinis are placed on cut-out torsos, these are then set against a fake marble background and floor. Colours are red, green, and white.

Above: a student display using white
models and suspended poles. Slotted
wall background adds to impact. Felt
covered shapes give solidity and throw
up the figures.

Left, above, and following page: in these pictures we can see the same prop used with a variety of merchandise. Display students were given the sculptured hands in an exercise where merchandise was the most important ingredient. The examples show clearly how a classic prop can adapt very easily and look right with a variety of goods. Hands were designed and made by Ivan Monty of Propaganza.

A Career in Display Design

Employment opportunities are quite diverse. Department stores generally employ quite large teams of personnel responsible for the display of products in windows and throughout the store. Multiple organisations have national networks of display teams organised regionally. Design studios involved in product promotion will also employ personnel with a display background to complement the promotional design team. In addition to what is essentially the selling side of display, it should be noted that museums and the public services are concerned with object and information presentation and in this sense, opportunities in the educational side of display should not be overlooked.

A typical career path in display would start at a junior appointment providing general assistance within a team, with progress through senior responsibilities for specific window and in-store promotions, supervising roles over a team or teams of display personnel, and then management functions overseeing all promotional activities within an organisation.

To ensure steady career progress, it is essential that records of work are maintained to support applications for further promotional opportunities. The British Display Society which seeks to promote the highest standards of display design within this country, offers grades of membership to reflect standards and levels of achievement among its members. To move through these grades, applications must be supported by a folio of work and details can be obtained from the Secretary at the address above.

Left: famous artists were the theme for this student assignment. Magritte was the inspiration for this display.
Above: students are continually given projects to sharpen their creative skills. The author provided them here with two simple cardboard plates. The picture shows how six students responded.

Associations

In England there are a number of organizations and trade associations which my readers might find helpful. America has a plethora of such bodies.

England
British Display Society
Guardian House
92–94 Foxberry Rd
London SE4 2SH

National Association of Shopfitters
412 Limpsfield Road
Warlingham, Surrey CR3 9HA

Shop and Display Equipment Association
24 Croydon Road
Caterham, Surrey CR3 6YR

America
Association of Visual Merchandise
Representatives
440 Molimo Dr.
San Francisco, CA 94127

Display Distributors Association
c/o The Nu-Era Group
727 N. 11th St.
St. Louis, MO 63101

The Display Guild
PO Box 87
W. Nyack, NY 10994

Left: these two figures were decorated and draped by students at The Grant McEwan College, Edmonton, Alberta, Canada. The theme was masquerade. Students first created the tissue paper wigs, then draped the dresses, made masks, and finally added the bows.

Institute of Store Planners
Jill Von Schlanbusch, President
211 E. 43rd St., 1601
New York, NY 10017

National Association of Store Fixture
Manufacturers
5975 W. Sunrise Blvd.
Sunrise, FL 33313

National Association of Display Industries
120 E. 23rd St., Third Floor
New York, NY 10010

National Retail Merchants Association
100 W. 31st St.
New York, NY 1001

Point-of-Purchase Advertising
Institute, Inc.
2 Executive Dr.
Fort Lee, NJ 07024

Society of Visual Merchandisers
PO Box 107
Madison Square Station
New York, NY 10159

The Western Association of Visual
Merchandising
27 Scott St.
San Francisco, CA 94117

Appendix

Whilst researching and writing this book I thought it would be interesting to contact a few professional people for whom I have a great respect within their chosen field. Not all are display names. Their comments or advice may seem obvious in some cases but sometimes the key to our art is to keep things simple while retaining impact and style. Students, then, should take note. This is how we should approach the whole subject of display or any creative work.

Ivan Monty   Ivan Monty is the one person I know in the display field who makes a nonsense out of the saying 'Jack of all trades, master of none'. For to me he has mastered so many as designer, painter, and display man. Now running his own business, Propaganza, he has brought his flair and expertise onto the prop market. Here are a few of his observations:

'I feel that we all of us take display too seriously for much of the time. Why can't we bring humour back into our work, let's give the customer a smile rather than a laugh. With the right approach and style we can do this with any merchandise. If we open our eyes and really look we can find that there is a lot of good young talent around, not only in London but all over the country. If I spot something that attracts or arrests my attention I like to let its creator know. We all need a boost and it is so easy to write a letter or phone. To young people, especially students, I would say, if you learn the rules through hard work and experience, you can then bend, even break them with assurance.'

Gene Moore   Gene Moore has been a leading figure in display circles for many years. I, and many other colleagues this side of the Atlantic, are always fascinated and amazed at the variety of his work for Tiffany & Co in the windows of their famous Fifth Avenue store. More than anyone else I can mention, Gene Moore links commerce, ideas, and lighting in his work, and turns them into entertainment. A man of few words and reluctant to air his views, he offered these words:

'I am not very good at giving advice concerning the world of display, however, the key word to me has always been awareness. Awareness of everything, of the past, the present, and one's own personal fantasy of the future.'

Paul Muller For some time I have known of Paul Muller's skills as group visual controller of Liberty, London, so I was delighted to have his views. He is never predictable, never resting on former successes, and I am in complete agreement with him on the merchandising aspects of display.

'The most important element in visual presentation is, I think, the balance between the merchandise and the display props. The props, though a necessary aid to selling merchandise, must not overpower it. Display has become much more business orientated. The merchandise is what matters. Therefore it is important that the visual managers work closely with the merchandise managers. All promotions, to be wholly effective, must be planned well in advance. Within this sharp business approach there is still room to lift the merchandise beyond itself and make it more appealing, more exciting. An art gallery exhibition, a film, or the theatre can provide the means. For example, the Liberty cotton promotion of 1984 was presented in pre-Raphaelite form to link with the pre-Raphaelite exhibition at the Tate Gallery. The result was an exciting display with enormous impact which in turn boosted sales.'

Adel Rootstein There can be few people working in display who have not heard of Adel Rootstein. Having worked in display herself she knew at first hand how important it was to any shop or store. She set her sights on the then very limited and basic ranges of display models. All this started to happen in the sixties when big changes were afoot in fashion. Creating more impactive store windows has been the Rootstein way of working since those early days. She strives continually to design and produce a product as close to the main stream of current fashion as sculpture and the materials used will allow. In her own words:

'Our success has come from modelling mannequins on real people, not on an idea of the average look. We use the mannequins to project the store's fashion image thus complementing the clothes displayed. Our aim is to instil a feeling of movement and direction into our mannequins therefore we are creating a definite statement.'

Ivan Tremayne Ivan Tremayne's contribution to the transformation that was happening at Sanderson had everyone talking. Cornish by birth, he had come from the West Country like a breath of fresh air on to the London display scene. Suddenly the showrooms sang with colour, huge urns spilled tumbling chintzes out onto the displays. Fabrics were knotted, swagged, wrapped, even draped on pre-Raphaelite figures. He always has an eye for a new technique or an exciting innovation.

'Every day people look at our displays and perhaps see something beyond the reflecting glass. Management hopes it is something to buy. In display we hope for something more with our ideas, moods, and schemes. Display often only promotes traditional tastes and values. Breaking new ground can be frowned upon, yet we must strive to keep up with a stream of new ideas. Management demands something new, but not too avant-garde. It has to be exciting, but not too outrageous. This is the challenge the display team faces. Despite all these restrictions placed upon the display artist, when creating a window he is, in the end, limited only by imagination.'

Janet Turner Janet Turner has been a friend and inspiration to me for many years. A perfectionist with feet firmly planted on the ground but eyes always seeking out the new, she approached the display situation with light as her main concern. She is Director of Concord Lighting.

'I feel that lighting is vital to all forms of display and decoration. It can breathe life into static objects or groups; reveal and enhance textures, colours, and patterns; and intensify or dramatize the beautiful or ordinary. I love to use light in all its forms — to play and experiment with the many effects and moods it can give us. To flood huge areas with brilliant light or pin point one rare object with a pencil beam. We can manipulate it in so many diverse ways: at the flick of a switch diamonds and crystal can sparkle and gleam, suede and stone reveal beautiful surface textures. We must not think of lighting as just an accessory, but as a fundamental part of our visual appreciation of all the many facets of display and presentation.

'There are several lighting situations that we see time and time again that I personally cannot stand. Areas flooded with bland lifeless light, this can turn any space into a clinical void. I hate to see spotlights glaring into our eyes, they not only blind us but look ugly and make viewing difficult if not impossible. Coloured lighting — like food colouring — needs to be used with tremendous care.'

Iris Webb   Iris Webb has not only been a personal friend of mine for many years but has encouraged and inspired many generations of men and women with her knowledge of flowers and foliage. Fascinated by the work of designers in display, theatre, and exhibitions, she writes here of her enduring passion for natural plant materials, a world closely linked with our own display one. Both areas have so much to learn from each other, and I am indebted to her for opening up yet another door to me. She is the Past President of the National Association of Flower Arrangement Societies (NAFAS).

'My sphere of display knowledge lies in the art or craft we know as flower arrangement — using flowers and foliage as a decoration in their own living natural form. Specialised knowledge is required of what colours, textures, shapes, and forms in flowers and leaves will achieve an effect that is visually right and pleasing to the viewer.

'All the known design principles apply. Great sensitivity to scale relationships, and choice of plant material is of particular importance. Flower arrangers are fully aware that they create only a fleeting beauty as do performers, dancers, and musicians. We are, as it were writing in sand. In many areas of display work our skills are used. Sometimes the decoration of tables, swags, and garlands, which we carry out in fresh flowers, has to be re-interpreted in dried or artificial materials. We lose that magical fresh quality but in many display situations living flowers are just not possible.'

Gary Withers Now the successful director of his own company, Imagination, Gary Withers is constantly exploring new and exciting ways to show products, new concepts, or rework the traditional. His is a working schedule that barely gives him time to touch down. He lives, breathes, and truly enjoys every aspect of display and decoration.

'At Imagination we handle display on a grand scale, re-shaping the environments in which we work. Whatever the size of the projects, they all have a common thread — the attention to detail. I believe that this is the key to all good display. Whether for a moment in time, as in the set for a television commercial, or on a more permanent basis with an exhibition, there is only one moment that counts. The first impression. Display is one of the most powerful commercial mediums available today. In reality it has moved far beyond the shop windows of our childhood to an ever widening palette of opportunity. Whilst man continues to manufacture and create, display lives, part of life and part of living. Its limits are limitless — only imagination is its boundary.'

Bibliography

Books on display and related topics

Allwood, John. *The Great Exhibition*. London: Studio Vista, 1977.

Berrall, Julia S. *A History of Flower Arrangement*. London: Thames & Hudson, 1969.

Cahan, Linda and Robinson, Joseph. *A Practical Guide to Visual Merchandising*. New York: Wiley, 1984.

Colborne, Robert. *Fundamentals of Merchandise Presentation*. Cincinnati: Signs of the Times, 1982.

Fuda, George E. and Nelson, Edwin L. *The Display Specialist*. New York: McGraw, 1976.

Gleeson, Ken, ed. *Interior Designer's Handbook*. London: Grosvenor Press, 1983.

Guild, Robert. *The Finishing Touch*. London: Marshall Editions, 1979.

Konikow, Robert B., ed. *Exhibit Design*. New York: PBC International, 1984.

Jacoby, Jacob and Olson, Jerry C, eds. *Perceived Quality: How Consumers View Stores and Merchandise*. Lexington: Lexington Books, 1984.

Marcus, Leonard. *The American Store Window*. New York: Watson-Gupthill, 1978.

Mauger, Emily M. *Modern Display Techniques*. New York: Fairchild, 1964.

Pegler, Martin M. *The Language of Store Planning and Display*. New York: Fairchild, 1981.

Pegler, Martin M. *Store Windows that Sell*. New York: Retail Reporting Bureau, 1980.

Pegler, Martin M. *Show and Sell*. Cincinnati: Signs of the Times, 1970.

Pegler, Martin M. *Visual Merchandising and Display*. New York: Fairchild, 1983.

Roth, Laszlo. *Display Design: An Introduction to the Art of Window Display*. New Jersey: Prentice Hall, 1983.

Samson, Harland and Little, Wayne G. *Display: Planning and Technique*. Cincinnati: South-Western Publishing, 1979.

Smith, Gary R. *Display and Promotion*. New York: McGraw, 1978.

Stanoch, Lenore, ed. *Display and Merchandising Idea Book*. Stamford: Progressive Grocer, 1982.

Turner, Janet, ed. *Light in Museums and Galleries*. London: Concord Lighting, 1985.

Varley, Helen, ed. *Colour*. London: Mitchell Beazley, 1980.

Wallick. *Display Manual for Libraries and Bookstores: Looking for Ideas?* New York: Scarecrow, Swinfen: Bailey Bros, 1970.

Wheeler, Alan. *Display: An Aid to Selling*. London: Heinemann, 1975.

Annuals

Annual of Display and Commercial Space Design in Japan. Japan: Rikuyo-sha Publishing.

The Creative Handbook. East Grinstead: Thomas Skinner Directories.

Stores of the Year. New York: Retail Reporting Bureau.

Periodicals on Display

Inspiration. Atlanta and London: Inspiration Press.

Retail Attraction. Eastcote (GB): AGB Business Publications.

Das Schaufenster. Passau: Verlag Passavia; London: Emgee Foreign Publications; New York: Museum Books; Thornhill: Ferro-Flex Canada.

Shop Equipment News. Eastcote: AGB Business Publications.

Store Planning Service. New York: Retail Reporting Bureau.

Visual Merchandising & Store Design. Cincinnati: Signs of the Times Publishing.

Periodicals on art and design
Art and Design. London: AD Editions.
Creative Review. London: Creative Review.
Design. London: Design Council.
Exhibition Bulletin. London: The London Bureau.
The Flower Arranger. London: National Association of Flower
    Arrangement Societies.
Graphis. Zurich and London: Graphis Press.
The World of Interiors. London: Conde Nast.
100 Idées. Paris: Marie Claire Album.

Index